Training Cross-C

This book was given to me by: _____

Here you can
put a photo
of yourself.

My name: _____

My birthday: _____

My address: _____

_____

TRAINING
CROSS-COUNTRY
SKIING

Katrin Barth & Hubert Brühl

Sports Science Consultant:
Dr. Berndt Barth

Meyer & Meyer Sport

Original Title: *Ich trainiere Skilanglauf*
© Aachen: Meyer & Meyer, 2005
Translated by Petra Haynes
AAA Translation, St. Louis, Missouri, USA
www.AAATranslation.com

British Library Cataloguing in Publication Data
A catalogue record for this book is available from the British Library

Training Cross-Country Skiing
Katrin Barth / Hubert Brühl
Oxford: Meyer & Meyer Sport (UK) Ltd., 2007
ISBN-10: 1-84126-196-3
ISBN-13: 978-1-84126-196-6

© 2007 by Meyer & Meyer Sport (UK) Ltd.
Aachen, Adelaide, Auckland, Budapest, Graz, Johannesburg,
New York, Olten (CH), Oxford, Singapore, Toronto
Member of the World
Sports Publishers' Association (WSPA)
www.w-s-p-a.org
Printed and bound by: B.O.S.S Druck und Medien GmbH, Germany
ISBN-10: 1-84126-196-3
ISBN-13: 978-1-84126-196-6
E-Mail: verlag@m-m-sports.com

TABLE OF CONTENTS

Please note:
The exercises and practical suggestions in this book have been carefully chosen and reviewed by the authors. However, the authors are not liable for accidents or damages of any kind incurred in connection with the content of this book.

HI, IT'S ME, LITTLE SNOWMAN! MAYBE YOU REMEMBER ME FROM THE BOOK "LEARNING SKIING."

ARE YOU READY FOR SOME SERIOUS TRAINING? OK, I'M WITH YOU!

HI, THERE, YOU SKI NUT! OF COURSE, I, BABY TIGER SKITTY AND FRIEND OF SNOWMAN, AM ONCE AGAIN ALONG FOR THE RIDE! I WOULDN'T MISS IT.

YOU WILL OFTEN SEE THESE SYMBOLS IN THIS BOOK

Whenever you see the thumb, we have a tip for you. You will receive suggestions or mistakes will be pointed out to you.

At this spot, you will find riddles or questions. The answers and solutions are in the back of the book.

In this book, you will find exercises you can easily do alone or at home.

When you see a pencil, it means there is something to color, fill in and complete.

. . . . 1 DEAR CROSS-COUNTRY SKIER

Many children, adolescents and adults consider skiing one of the best recreational activities in winter. Exercise in the fresh, clear winter air feels good and is healthy. Many children, particularly in the mountains, take learning to ski for granted. It is something you have to learn how to do, just like walking, swimming or riding a bike. Because you learned the basics of skiing, you can now propel yourself forward on skis, manage to get up an incline, control your direction and speed going downhill, and you can definitely stop at will.

If you are now interested in this training book and reading it, we can assume that to you cross-country skiing is not simply "sliding through the forest." You enjoy this sport, want to continue on and train seriously. You want to keep getting faster, refine your cross-country skiing technique, improve your fitness level and successfully compete in competitions. You want to get incredible times and win. You might already be a member of a ski club or ski group and might be training with your peers under the direction of experienced trainers or ski instructors.

BUT FIRST A LITTLE STORY:

A strapping boy was visiting the mountains and wanted to climb a high peak. Cheerfully, he packed food and drink, and started to hike with a bounce in his step.

Since he wasn't familiar with the route, he made slow progress. He climbed up and when he realized that he couldn't get any further, he had to turn back and start over. These detours cost him lots of strength. Sometimes he got lucky and found a trail that brought him a little closer to the top. After many such attempts, he finally reached the summit, only to realize that others were already there. They told him about a good hiking trail. He could have taken that without all those detours.

Why didn't he use a map or ask someone who had already taken this hike?

Ski training is similar to our story about the "conqueror of the peaks." Many cross-country skiers before you have trained and some have become very successful. You don't have to reinvent cross-country skiing and ski training, but rather learn from the experiences of athletes before you. It will make it much easier for you.

This training book "Training Cross-Country Skiing" will provide you with a kind of "trail map" and a tutorial on how you can climb the "skiers peak" without making a lot of detours. And, of course, there's your trainer who can also show you the right way to train.

It sometimes happens that experienced skiers, trainers and book writers have slightly different opinions with regard to training. That is normal. Ask if you are not clear on something and find out the reasons behind different opinions. If we are mistaken or the development has simply progressed, make a note directly in your book.

But before you go to bed at night with this book under your pillow, thinking that's how you will win tomorrow:

We want to help you and explain how you can train properly. But you must train on your own. Whether or not you reach your goal and make it to the peak is mainly up to you.

Anything in this book pertaining to training applies to girls, as well as boys. But to keep it simple, we will refer to skiers or athletes in general. That means that trainer of course also refers to female trainers.

We hope you have lots of fun with this book. It will certainly provide you with lots of interesting information to accompany you on a hopefully quick and safe trip to the top. We wish you lots of success!

The authors, Snowman and Skitty.

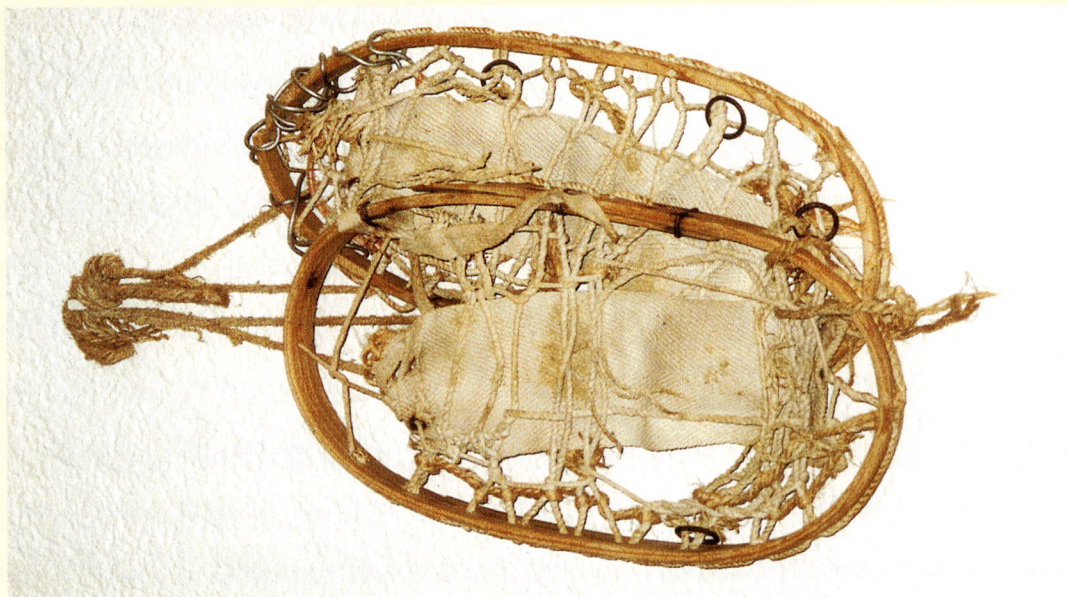

These are snowshoes like those worn by ancient peoples during long walks and hunts in the snow.

These are wooden skis with bindings made from leather straps. The poles are made from bamboo.

. . . . 2 FROM WOODEN SKIS TO SKATE SKIS

Which people skied first? Who built the first skis? Was it the Native Americans, the northern Germanic tribes or the Stone Age people in what is now the Sahara desert?

Of course, no one can say for sure, but they definitely were people who wanted to survive and move around in the snow. Snowshoes were constructed using twigs or hewn from pieces of wood. One no longer had to laboriously trudge through the snow, but was now able to move faster, and thus be more successful in hunting.

It did not take long before people began to enjoy moving around in their wintry surroundings and gliding downhill fast. Maybe they even held small contests and races. Of course, the materials and the technique always changed and improved. And that still continues today!

Sometimes you can see old snow shoes, skis or poles as decorations in ski huts or lodges.

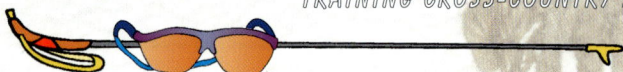

DID YOU KNOW ...

...THAT ANCIENT ROCK PAINTINGS HAVE BEEN FOUND THAT SHOW HUNTERS ON SKIS HUNTING REINDEER?
THE FIRST STONE AGE DRAWINGS DATE BACK TO APPROXIMATELY 4,000 B.C.

... THAT PEOPLE IN NORTHERN EUROPE WORSHIPPED SKI GODS?
THERE WAS ULL OR ULLR, FOR WHOM MANY NORWEGIAN TOWNS ARE STILL NAMED TODAY.
THE NORTHERN COUNTRIES IN EUROPE WERE EVEN NAMED SKANDINAVIA, AFTER THE SKIING GODDESS SKADI.

... THAT FOR A LONG TIME CROSS-COUNTRY SKIING HAD NOTHING TO DO WITH SPORTS? IT WAS SIMPLY A WAY OF GETTING AROUND IN SNOW AND ICE AND TO HUNT.

... THAT IN 1888-1889 THE FAMOUS NORWEGIAN POLAR EXPLORER, FRIDTJOF NANSEN, WAS THE FIRST TO TRAVERSE GREENLAND?
HE AND HIS COMPANIONS WERE PRACTICED SNOWSHOERS AND MADE GOOD PROGRESS WITH THE SKIS. HIS BOOK ABOUT THE EXPEDITION IMPRESSED MANY PEOPLE BACK THEN AND GOT THEM INTERESTED IN SKIING.

... THAT FOR A LONG TIME TWO SKIS OF DIFFERENT LENGTHS WERE USED?
THE SHORTER SKI HAD FUR ON THE TREAD, WHICH THE SKIER USED TO PUSH OFF WITH. THE LONGER SKI WAS FOR GLIDING.

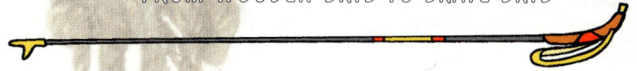

... THAT CROSS-COUNTRY SKIERS INITIALLLY USED ONLY ONE POLE FOR SUPPORT? WHEN THE USE OF TWO POLES FINALLY PERSEVERED, THIS TECHNIQUE WAS CRITICIZED BY SOME AS BEING UNATTRACTIVE AND UNPRACTICAL. "THE SKIERS HANG ON TWO POLES AND WADDLE THROUGH THE COUNTRYSIDE!"

... THAT THE FOUNDER OF MODERN IN-SCHOOL PHYSICAL EDUCATION, JOHANN CHRISTOPH GUTSMUTHS, WAS HIMSELF A SKIER AROUND 1800 AND RECOMMENDED SKIING AS A VALUABLE PHYSICAL EXERCISE? HE BECAME THE FOUNDER OF SKIING IN GERMANY.

... THAT THE FIRST OLYMPIC WINTER GAMES WERE HELD IN 1924?

... THAT MANY YEARS AGO THERE WAS AN ADVERTISING SLOGAN FOR CROSS-COUNTRY SKIING? IT SAID: "CROSS-COUNTRY SKIERS LIVE LONGER."

... THAT IN 1974, THURINGIAN GERHARD GRIMMER BECAME THE FIRST GERMAN WORLD CHAMPION IN CROSS-COUNTRY SKIING? ONLY 29 YEARS LATER, IN 2003, WAS AXEL TEICHMANN ABLE TO ACHIEVE THE SAME INCREDIBLE RESULT.

... THAT NORWAY IS THE MOST SUCCESSFUL CROSS-COUNTRY SKIING NATION WITH THE MOST OLYMPIC CHAMPIONS AND WORLD CHAMPIONS?

THE EVOLUTION OF CROSS-COUNTRY SKIING TECHNIQUE

Even in the Middle Ages, the Norwegian wild bird hunters on their thin boards were faster than their game. The polar explorer Fridtjof Nansen traversed Greenland on snowshoes in the late 19th century. This was called "walking on the plain." We found the following simple description of cross-country ski technique in an old ski book[1]:

"... one straps on one's two narrow boards and is off in a relaxed gliding stride across broad plains, through forest, around trees and turns, through valleys and dells snow covered with winter's magical cloak."

The skating stride was already well known and inclines were mastered with the herringbone stride. The cross-country ski sport later developed the classical racing techniques, like the diagonal stride, double poling with or without kick, and step turning.

The skating techniques with technical models and technical descriptions were added in the more recent past. There continue to be refinements and improvements to get faster. Perhaps you have heard of the Siitonen technique, the Three-phase, the symmetrical (V1) or the asymmetrical (V2) skate.

---

[1] "Ski School From A-Z" (1942) Lantschner & Harster, Munich: Knorr & Hürth

HOW IS CROSS-COUNTRY SKIING ORGANIZED?

Most athletes in ski training are members of a club. There they have the best training conditions, certified trainers and good physical care. It is fun to prepare with one's training buddies for an athletic competition and to start for the team.

What is the name of your club? Write the name down here and paste in or draw the logo and club colors.

My club: *Logo:*

_____

_____

Every country has a national organization for its ski athletes.

Do you know the name of your national association?
Write it down here.

_____

A national ski association supports clubs, attends to the training of ski instructors and trainers, looks after the top athletes and holds competitions and championships in the various disciplines. In addition, it also serves recreational athletes, supports the work in ski areas and organizes contests for children and adolescents.

HOW SKIING IS ORGANIZED AT THE INTERNATIONAL LEVEL

The worldwide association for all ski athletes is called the **Fédération International de Ski** (FIS).

The FIS was founded at the first Winter Olympics in Chamonix, France in 1924. It has been based in Oberhofen, Switzerland for many years.

All national ski associations are members of the FIS. There are currently more than 103 member nations. There are committees for alpine ski sports, cross-country skiing, Nordic Combined, ski jumping, Freestyle and snowboarding. These also have subcommittees.

Their tasks include:

❄ Making decisions regarding rules, materials and dates.

❄ Responsibility for the awarding and implementation of the big World Cup races.

❄ The advancement and modernization of the popular World Cup disciplines in ski and snowboard sports, particularly the cross-country ski competitions.

The FIS is the organizer of the ski and snowboard World Championships and is responsible for the ski and snowboard competitions at the Olympic Games.

If you want to know more, look on the Internet:

www.fis-ski.com

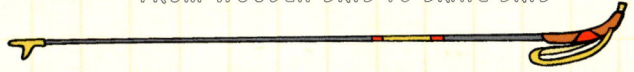

THE LIST OF CURRENT WORLD CHAMPIONS

It is interesting to keep track of which athletes are the best. Record your favorite distance here and write down the winners. You can also keep such overviews for other distances.

	Distance	
World Champion	2007	
	2009	
Olympic Champion	2006	
	2010	
World Cup Winner	2006	
	2007	
	2007	

SPORT AND ART

Sports and athletes are popular themes for many artists. Many paintings, drawings, sculptures, and photographs have been and are inspired by the elegance of the movement, the beauty of the body, the speed and the strength of skiers.

Have you ever seen such a piece of sports art? Look for them whenever you are in a public building or a museum.

Helga Borisch
"Staffelwechsel"
("Handoff")
(1980)

Hans Erni
"Cross-county Skiing"
(1983)

3 HI THERE, AXEL TEICHMANN!

Axel Teichmann
Born July 14, 1979
In Ebersdorf, Thuringia (Germany)
World Champion 2003

Hi Axel! What do you think is so great about cross-country skiing?

To walk alone through the snowy woods on cold, sunny days, enjoying wonderful nature – that is an amazing experience. Cross-country skiing is a sport you can practice in the open air. It is a way to be close to nature.

What abilities does a good cross-country skier need?

A good cross-country skier needs endurance, strength and muscle sense for the cross-country skiing technique. This is partly inherent but mostly the result of years of diligent training. In order to advance one's abilities and skills, one has to continuously overcome one's weaker inner self. A successful cross-country skier must be able to do that.

Do you sometimes not feel like training? What do you do then?

Of course I don't always feel like training. But I have many goals, and I know what I want to accomplish. Big goals can only be achieved through regular training. Training together with friends in my training group is very helpful. No one likes going out there in bad weather by himself. But when I really don't feel like doing it and I don't feel well, then it's better to take a break. Better to rest up and start anew, than to do only a halfway decent job.

What were your greatest and most important successes?

My greatest and most important success was the title of World Champion in 2003, in the 15 km classic style in Val di Fiemme, Italy. After my two gold medals in the Junior World Championships I was able to prove that I could make it to the top of the podium with the men, too. I was able to fulfill the high expectations others have had of me for years.

What goals do you still have?

I want to become individual World Champion one more time and win World Championship gold with the relay team. My biggest goal is a medal at the Olympics.

Do you also have other interests?

In my free time, I enjoy computers and technical gadgets.

The computer also allows me to document my training and competition results and thereby track my performance development. I am also passionate about playing soccer, and three years ago I started sport climbing and bouldering. Climbing is an incredible challenge for body and mind. You are out in nature undisturbed and constantly have to solve new tasks in the rock.

What tips do you have for young athletes?

The experiences you have in the sport and in the club can often help you in other areas of your life. I would not want to miss that. In the club, you make many new friends with whom you can train and go to competitions. You will have lots of fun and many a joyful celebration together.

THANK YOU VERY MUCH FOR THE INTERVIEW AND LOTS OF LUCK IN THE FUTURE!

FAN PAGE

Which successful skier would you like to interview?

_____

What question would you ask him or her?

_____

_____

_____

Here you can paste photos of your idols or collect autographs.

. . . . 4 TRAINING –
THE RIGHT WAY TO SUCCESS

To ski and skate like the top athletes would be the best! You want to be fast and powerful. You want to make precious time on the inclines with your perfect technique and barely have to break on the complicated downhill stretches.

Maybe you have noticed during training and at competitions that things don't always go as perfectly as you would like. Perhaps, also your cross-country skiing technique isn't quite that good just yet, you have trouble with challenging courses, on steep inclines and fast downhill stretches. You might be unsure in changing snow conditions. Also, you might have noticed that others can ski pretty well, too. Some are even faster than you.

But not to worry! No one was ever born a champion skier! The others had to start the same way you did and have only gotten this far with lots of training.

But what can you do to become a good, and maybe even top, skier?

With this training book, we want to help you train successfully.

THE PATH TO THE SKI SUMMIT

The book won't be able to replace your trainer, but it will explain why your trainer works on technique and body conditioning with you, and why he says that you need to improve your endurance, co-ordination, strength and flexibility.

You will learn to understand why it is necessary to do summer training and training in the gym in addition to snow training in winter.

You will recognize how important it is to warm up and stretch before training and before a race. And you find out why you sometimes think you can't do any better and why you are not equally good every day.

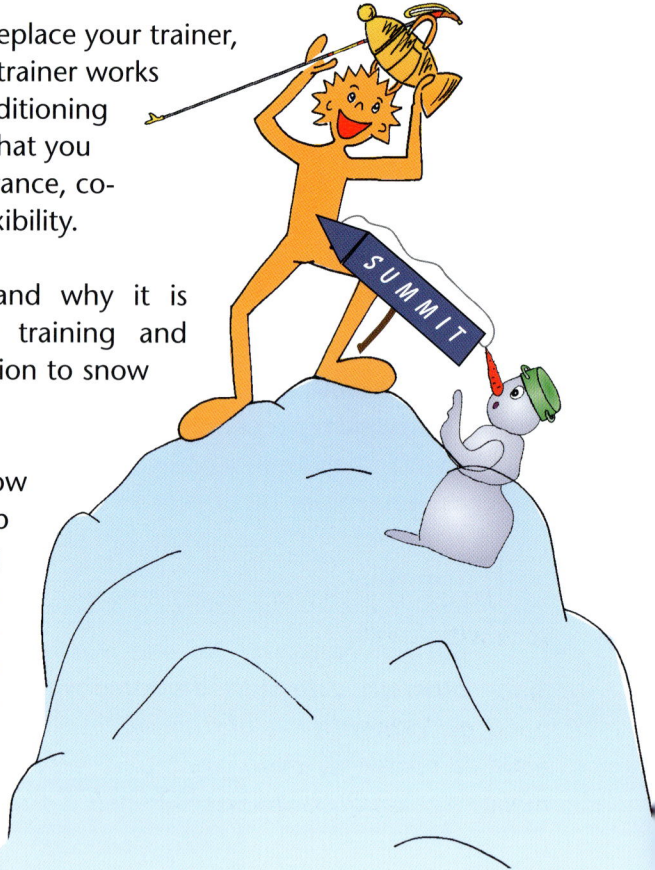

In addition, you will get suggestions on what you can do yourself, in training and outside of the regular training sessions, to improve your performance and independently monitor and evaluate your progress. The top skiers do that. After many years of training and many races they know exactly whether or not they are in shape and what they have to work on to get even better.

To the athlete, the trainer then becomes a good friend and counselor who sometimes also has to be strict when the "weaker inner self" says, "That's just too hard today. I quit!"

TRAINING ACTIVELY AND CONSCIOUSLY

Anything one has to **actively** and **consciously** do to get better at cross-country skiing is considered cross-country ski training. But what does that mean?

Active means that you yourself have to train. You don't get better by having your trainer tackle the course and ski all those miles. Only by actually training yourself, or by being active, will you improve.

Consciously means that you understand the purpose and benefit of the tasks the trainer gives you and carry them out independently. You may also think up training tasks of your own and carry them out.

You should not only do what you are told, but you should also know why you are doing it. That is good for your success. When you know why you are doing something, you enjoy it more and stick with it longer.

Since a cross-country skier has to train many years to achieve good performances, it makes sense to find out at the beginning what it means to train right and learn how to train. You will make more progress and training will be much more fun.

TRAINING RIGHT – BUT HOW?

By answering these three questions, you can see if you are ready for training:

1 **What** do I want to achieve?

2 **Why** do I want to train?

3 **How** can I train to reach my goals?

1 What do I want to achieve? What are my training goals?

Active and conscious training require specific goals. If you don't have a goal, training soon won't be fun anymore because you won't know why you are working so hard. A cross-country skier's most important goal is to enjoy skiing. But, in the long term, it will only be fun if you get a better feel for the pace, the skis and the snow, and are able to master any terrain – even in varying snow conditions – with a versatile ski technique. Then you will get good results in races and continue to perform better in comparison with other skiers.

Or would you like to always be the slowest one and lose?

Maybe you set a really big goal right away. The Olympic competitions are shown on television or you are watching a World Cup race. The skiers are intensely focused and technically perfect. They reach the finish line in record time. Everyone cheers, marvels and is thrilled. You think, "I want to do that, too."

And that's the way it should be! But you do have to bear in mind that dreaming of success doesn't make it real. It will take lots of sweat first, and along with some small successes, you will suffer many defeats along the way.

Next to the big goals that are still off in the distant future, you should also set some short-term goals. For example, you might resolve to perfect your skiing technique, to master the inclines more easily, and to cheat less during fitness training.

Goals are the impetus of every ambitious athlete!

It is fun to reach the goals you have set, and when that doesn't happen it is an incentive. However, don't set impossible goals for yourself, but only ones that are realistic and that you can reach in the near future.

DOESN'T THE TRAINER HAVE TO SET THE GOALS?

Maybe you think that it is the trainer's job. He can tell you what you can and should achieve. He will do that. He sets training goals for his athletes and designs training plans and trains with them according to these plans.

But every skier knows himself best, knows his strengths and weaknesses. That is why he also knows which goals to set for himself. It is always better to set your own goals than have them "pressed on you" by someone else. Then they are your own goals and you are much more willing to do everything to achieve them. If you can tell your trainer exactly what isn't working so well yet and what you want to really work on in the near future, then he can respond by helping you train.

WHAT'S THIS?

COACH, I HAVE TO LOOK UP MY NEXT TRAINING GOAL!

Imagine yourself in the following situations while training with a new trainer. How would you react?

1 *Your trainer tells you to complete a 0.5 km loop with a steep incline five consecutive times at competition-like speed with only a brief break. It is too much for you because, due to a bad cold, you have not been able to practice for a long time.*

2 *The snow and track conditions are ideal. The trainer asks that you spend the entire training session practicing step turns to the left and the right in one area of the ski meadow, but the directional changes did not give you any trouble in the last race.*

Write your goals along with the date in the following chart on page 31. In the second column, add the date you want to achieve the goal by. Once you have actually achieved it, you can check it off and write down the real date.

When the list is full, draw a new chart and lay or paste it in the book. But you can also start a "goal notebook" that you can use over a longer period of time.

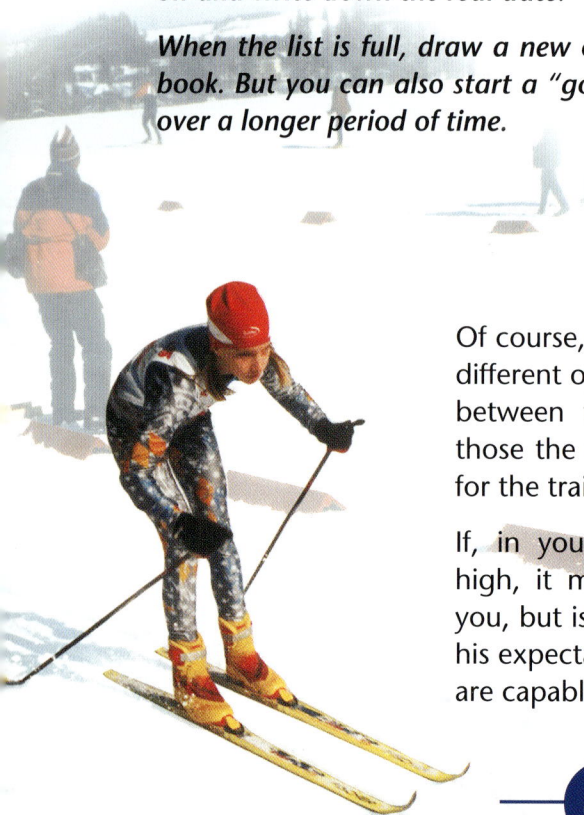

Of course, trainers and athletes sometimes have different opinions. In part, there is inconsistency between the goals you set for yourself and those the trainer envisions for you. It isn't easy for the trainer.

If, in your opinion, his expectations are too high, it means he has a lot of confidence in you, but is asking too much of you. If you think his expectations are too low, show him that you are capable of more.

What I want to achieve/Date		Target date/ Made it!	
To do the 1,000 m in less than	/ 12.22	(01.08) 01.16	✓
To be able to do .... push-ups	/ 02.07	(02.07)	

THE OVERALL GOAL AND SUB-GOALS

At the last competition, Tom was not able to place at the top. He did not meet the expectations of the trainer, the training group, the club, his parents, or his own. But he also knows the reason, which is namely his lack of strength endurance on long inclines.

He has resolved to improve his strength endurance in training during the course of the year. That is his overall goal, but he won't be able to achieve everything during the first few training sessions. That is why he has set sub-goals that will help him to achieve his overall goal.

Here you can see what that means:

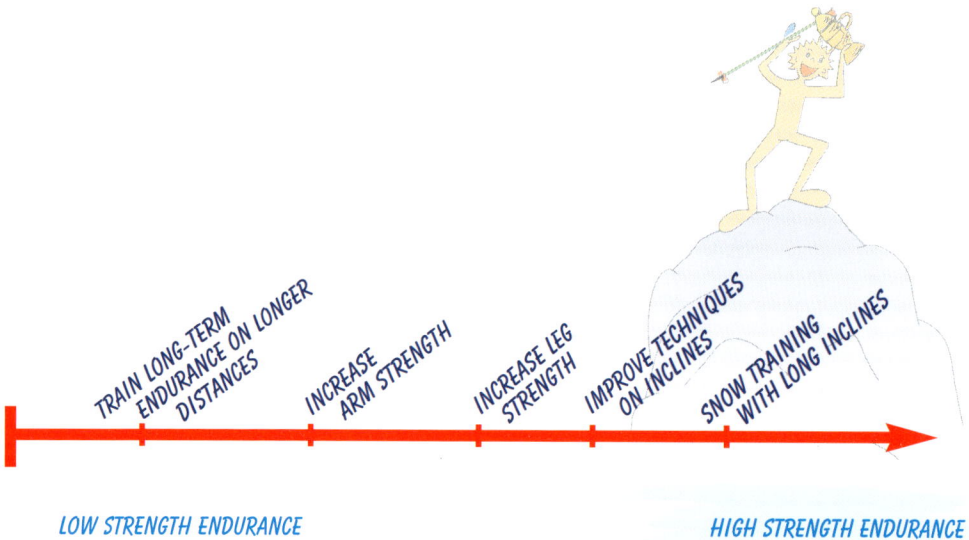

TRAIN LONG-TERM ENDURANCE ON LONGER DISTANCES

INCREASE ARM STRENGTH

INCREASE LEG STRENGTH

IMPROVE TECHNIQUES ON INCLINES

SNOW TRAINING WITH LONG INCLINES

LOW STRENGTH ENDURANCE

HIGH STRENGTH ENDURANCE

This is how you can set sub-goals for all fitness-related abilities, for cross-country skiing techniques, for competitive strength, etc., and then you can be pleased when you have made it.

2 Why do I want to train for cross-country skiing? What is the reason for my training? What are the motives?

The reason, or the *motive,* for training is the "psychological motor" that initiates the training. They determine whether or not you go to practice, whether you fight or just give up when you fail.

Going to practice is never a problem when the weather is nice and you are bored. You want to get out into the fresh winter air and enjoy the white snow and the forest. There you get to see your friends, and your coach may have something exciting planned. But what happens when it rains, when there isn't enough snow yet, and with all that yucky weather there is great show on television? Or on a beautiful summer day, when your school buddies are at the ice cream parlor or at the pool? Are you as quick to get your gym bag packed on those days as well? But if you really want to reach a sub-goal, and you know that the next training session is particularly important for the new season or the upcoming competition, then the decision won't be that tough.

I AM GOING TO PRACTICE AND TRY TO DO MY BEST ...

	Very important reason	Important reason	Not that important
Because I love winter and snow.	☐	☐	☐
Because I want to do something for my health.	☐	☐	☐
Because I want to ski as well as my idol.	☐	☐	☐
Because my parents want me to.	☐	☐	☐
Because my friend is going, too.	☐	☐	☐
Because I don't want to disappoint my trainer.	☐	☐	☐
Because I enjoy being in a great training group.	☐	☐	☐
Because I don't have anything else to do.	☐	☐	☐
Because I love competing on the track.	☐	☐	☐
Because I love the race against the clock.	☐	☐	☐
Because I want to be in the paper.	☐	☐	☐
Because I want to make the national team.	☐	☐	☐
Because I am building character through training.	☐	☐	☐
Because cross-country skiing is just awesome.	☐	☐	☐
Because _____	☐	☐	☐
Because _____	☐	☐	☐

Reevaluate why you go to practice and work hard. Decide how important a motive is to you. Make an X in the appropriate column of the list on page 34. If you have any other motives, add them on the two blank lines.

The coach says to Max, "Ski the course as fast as you can!" Max does his best and is pretty pleased with his performance.

Tina skies after him. The trainer clocks a better time for her. That annoys Max, who had been quite pleased with his result. Now Max wants to compete against Tina directly because that defeat is tough to swallow.

In principle, the final result isn't important because, as you can imagine, Max completed the course faster than before. Competing against Tina had directly motivated him to ski even faster.

A very important reason for exerting yourself in training is knowing why you have to do the individual exercises, and how doing them will help you improve your performance.

Anything you do with interest goes twice as well!

3 How can I train so I will reach my goals? In what way can I improve my performance through training?

In training, the exertion that is supposed to lead to improved performance is called load. Just like every skier is different, so is his load capacity and the load required for an improved performance. If an athlete does not sufficiently exert himself in training, he will not achieve an improvement in performance, and when his load is too high, it can

lead to exhaustion and to injuries due to a lack of concentration. Unfortunately, there is no chart to tell the skier or trainer how high the load should or can be. Every athlete has to help determine that for himself. Over time, he will learn to listen to his body and recognize when the load is high enough. The proper training load will lead to a performance increase because our bodies adapt. Thus the heart gets larger and more efficient, the muscles get stronger, and you are able to fully concentrate for a longer period of time. After a period of regular training, you will notice that the exercises that used to get you winded aren't nearly as strenuous anymore. If you used to get totally exhausted on your training course, you will be able to hang in there a lot longer.

Many sports scientists and doctors have done tests and research to determine which training methods are most beneficial for cross-country skiers to bring about the best athletic performance and keep the body healthy and fit. Just training usually doesn't bring the desired success. It can even hurt you.

Surely you have noticed that your performance drops when you don't practice for a while. At the first training session after a break, the motion sequences and exercises probably seemed more difficult and your performance wasn't as good.

WHAT'S THIS?

SHHH, COACH! I'M TRYING TO HEAR IF MY BODY CAN HANDLE A FEW MORE EXERCISES!

So you had to start over with a lesser load than what you had finished the last training session with. We will go into that again in chapter 9, "Training Plan."

Regular training is better than irregular training!

Do you remember our example about the goal you want to reach? Laziness and inconsistency in training interrupt performance development. You are thrown backward on the path to success. It is as if you were sliding back part of the distance you've already covered.

But often it isn't possible to train as hard as you had planned. There are times when you have to study more for school or you are on vacation with your parents. Maybe there isn't enough snow or available gym time.

When someone sets a goal for athletic performance, he has to train regularly. That includes endurance exercise, strength training and calisthenics. If you are not able to train due to illness or injury, you definitely have to rest and get well. But if you are not able to go to practice because of vacation, a school event or for other reasons, then try to still stay in shape.

Go jogging, do some strength exercises or stretches indoors, or work on your flexibility. Also use the summer to improve your strength and endurance through swimming, paddling, inline skating or mountain biking. That will make catching up after the break a little easier.

WHAT MAKES A GOOD CROSS-COUNTRY SKIER?

Surely you can think of many good answers to this question. There is a lot a good cross-country skier must possess, know and be able to do. In this chart, we attempt to illustrate everything that impacts the performance of a ski athlete and what has to be trained. The individual factors definitely cannot be viewed independently of each other. That is why in the illustration the circles also overlap. The circle of psychological abilities surrounds everything because they affect everything. In addition, there are important exterior influences, which you can see by the outer arrows.

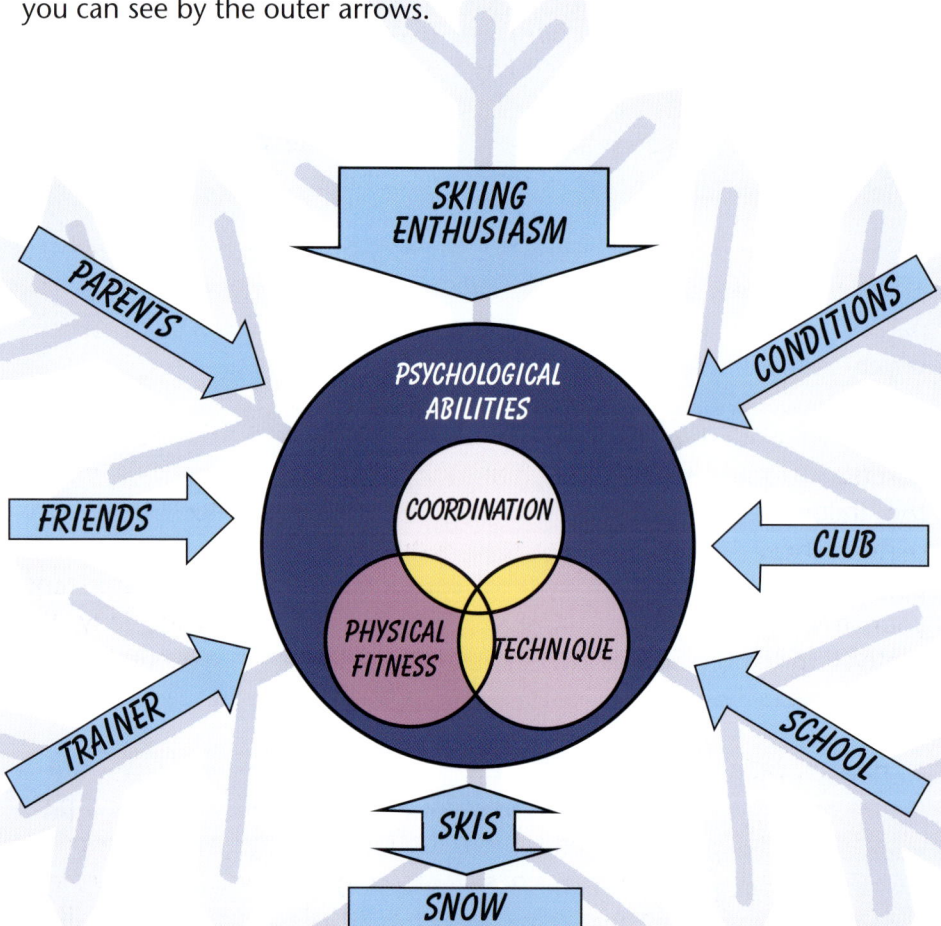

SKIING ENTHUSIASM

PARENTS

CONDITIONS

FRIENDS

CLUB

TRAINER

SCHOOL

PSYCHOLOGICAL ABILITIES

COORDINATION

PHYSICAL FITNESS

TECHNIQUE

SKIS

SNOW

Technique refers to the movements that are typical in cross-country skiing. These include pushing off, gliding, poling, changing direction, downhill and uphill technique.

A cross-country skier who has good endurance and strength, speed and flexibility, is said to have a high level of **physical fitness**. A race and an entire competition require lots of strength and stamina. You have to be totally fit and focused during the entire time.

While skiing at a fast pace, a constant alternating between pushing off, gliding, tensing and relaxing of muscles takes place. Depending on the technique, the leg and arm work must be perfectly coordinated. You constantly have to adjust to the routing and the snow conditions. **Coordination** is very important here.

How confident, strong or timid you are, whether you are discouraged or spurred on to really fight when someone passes you or if you choose the wrong wax, depends on your **psyche**.

Our chart also shows arrows that include **parents, friends, trainer, conditions, club and school.** (One could easily add more.) Those are the influences that come from the outside and affect the skier's performance. It matters greatly whether the parents support your training or are against it. How well you get along with the trainer and your training buddies is also significant. And who can deny the motivating force of a blue sky and sunshine, and fresh, glittering snow? Problems at school or family stress do not allow for a clear head.

It makes a difference whether many spectators are cheering, the sun is shining and you like your new suit, or no one pays attention to you, the run is slushy, your boots pinch and the old skis aren't gliding well. And without the necessary **skiing enthusiasm** you won't likely achieve a top performance.

All factors combined bring success

Cross-country skiing is demanding in terms of endurance and strength endurance. That is why physical fitness is so important. But you can't win races with physical fitness alone. And if all you have is perfect technique or amazing coordination, everyone else will still pass you up. A cross-country skier must have it all. And when our control system – the psyche – fails us, everything can go topsy-turvy. But it is very difficult to build up all of the components at the same time. Therefore, in order to become a successful skier, you have to train everything bit by bit.

What does that mean in regard to your training?

The best way to improve your physical fitness, coordination and technique is through training. Spending more time on skis or inline skates naturally improves your chances for making progress in training. But if you notice a particular weakness in one area, additional training will be necessary. In the following chapters, we will address the individual factors in more detail and discuss training methods. We will show you some options for exercises you can do at home, for self-monitoring and evaluation of your own performance. Discuss everything with your trainer, as well. He knows the ropes.

GREAT, JULIE! I'M ECSTATIC! TODAY YOU SKIED LIKE A FUTURE WORLD CHAMPION!

BUT COACH, THAT'S A NO-BRAINER! I HAVE NEW SKIS, THE SNOW IS EXCELLENT, AND MY PARENTS ARE ROOTING FOR ME.

YESTERDAY I RECEIVED THE BEST REPORT CARD EVER AND I MADE UP WITH MY FRIEND TINA.

BESIDES, I HAVE A CRUSH ON TOM! ANYTHING ELSE?

. . . . 5 MENTAL ABILITIES

Why is it that humans can feel joy and sadness, that they can fall in love or hate someone? Why are people able to think, remember and dream?

People have always been curious about what goes on inside their bodies. No one had an explanation, so they called the whole thing the *soul.* The famous physician Rudolf Virchow (1821-1902) once asked his students to find the soul in the human body. But what they found inside the bodies they dissected were the brain, the heart, the lungs, the liver, and all of the other organs. They did not find a soul.

Of course, they could not have found it, because our ability to perceive, imagine, think, decide, feel and want are the result of our brain's activity. The science that deals with this is called psychology, and the old term soul was replaced by the word psyche.

Thus mental, or *psychological,* abilities refer to the skier's ability to handle joy, anger, rage, excitement, competitiveness, fear and the many other emotions, and to advantageously and successfully apply them in training and during competitions. In psychology, research is also being done on how the thinking process works and how our muscles receive commands. We imagine our brain as a computer that controls everything. While you are skiing, your "computer" is working at high capacity, which is why it needs to be well prepared.

WHAT DOES OUR "COMPUTER" LOOK LIKE ON THE INSIDE?

We don't want to turn this into a medical lecture. Besides, the brain as a topic is much too complicated and extensive to cover in a short chapter. But some people really think that sports are just about muscles. They don't know that the muscles' impulses originate in the brain, and that every complex athletic movement and action is controlled by nerve connections in the brain.

SKIN EARS

EYES

MUSCLES

TONGUE

In order for you to understand the importance of your brain in skiing, we could not leave a chapter like this out of this training book.

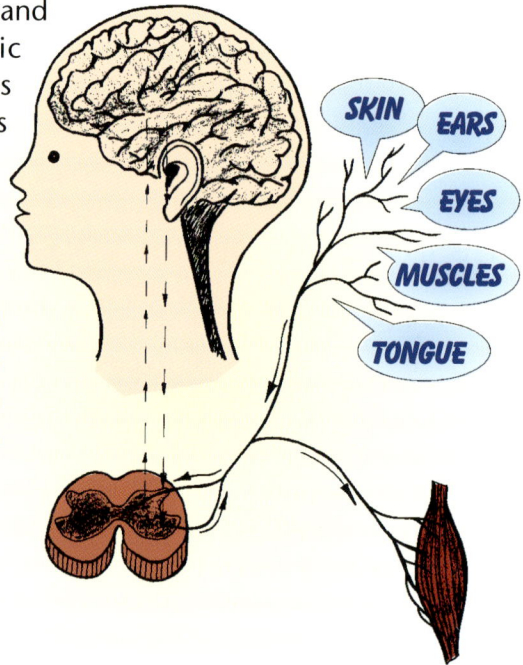

PERCEPTION – CIRCUIT – BRAIN – MUSCLE

The illustrations show a simplified version of how this process works. You receive lots of information via receptors located in your sensory organs. You can see, hear, taste and feel things.

Nerve tracts then carry this information to the brain. On the way to the brain the information first ends up at a circuit. In our illustration, this is a piece of bone marrow located in the spinal column. The brain then sends an "order" to the respective muscle, telling it what to do.

INCOMING INFORMATION FOR THE BRAIN: I SEE SOMETHING YELLOW AND IT IS VERY HOT!

JUST A MOMENT, I'LL CONNECT!

IT COULD BE THE SUN, AND IT IS DANGEROUS! ORDER TO MUSCLES: QUICKLY GET IN THE SHADE!

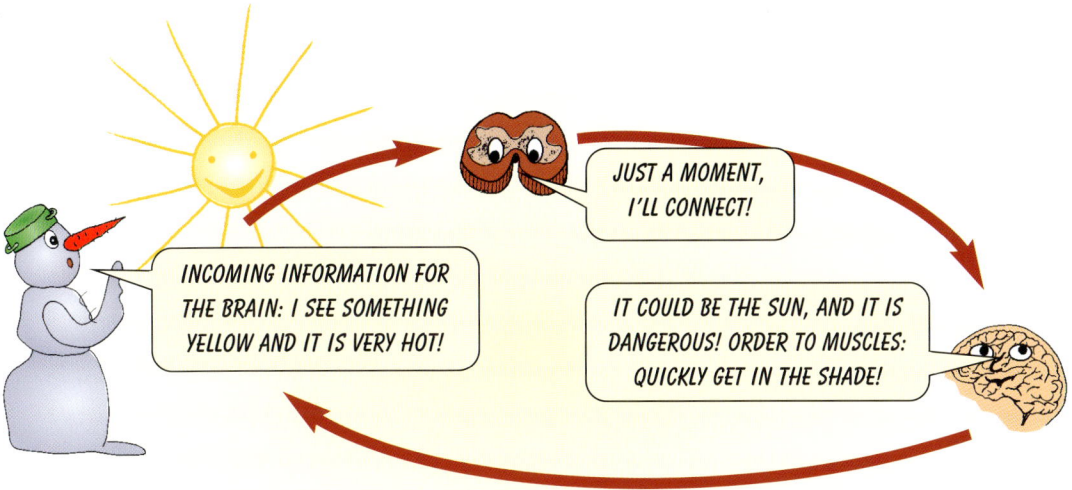

Conscious reaction

Most impulses and information we receive via our senses are relayed from the circuits to the appropriate section of the brain. After the incoming impulses are checked, they are compared with experiences and mentally processed. The orders travel along the nerve tracts from the cerebral cortex via the spinal cord (that was the circuit) to the muscles for the execution of the conscious actions.

An example:

❄ *Incoming impulse:*
You are skiing at a high speed and see a sharp turn coming up.

❄ *Compare with experiences:*
You know that if you don't get into a tuck and decrease your speed, you may crash. That would cost you lots of time.

❄ *Mental preparation:*
Build-up body tension, slight plow position, tighten muscles, crouch, use upper body to create counterpoise.

Pretty difficult! But don't worry, most of this will come easily when you have trained properly and have gained some experience.

1 Building a snowman: Find 11 differences!

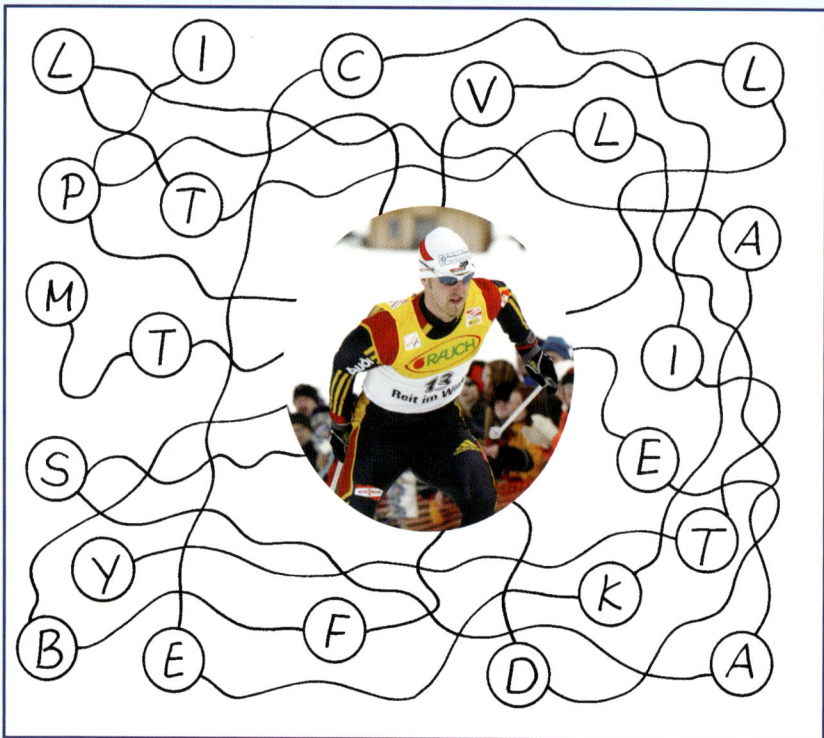

2 Hidden here is a city that once hosted the Winter Olympics. You will find its name by finding the correct start of the track and then continuing to follow the 12 letters.

Reflexes

Are you familiar with the following situations? You accidentally touch a hot stove top and quickly pull your hand away, or you are blinded by bright light and squeeze your eyes shut, or you slip on a slick surface and flail your arms to keep from falling. In these situations, your muscles react automatically, without your having to think about what to do. This reaction is called reflex. Because you don't have to first think about what to do, the information does not have to be forwarded to the brain. The impulse goes from the circuit straight to the muscle.

In cross-country skiing, these phenomena occur when, for instance, you suddenly begin to slide or lose your balance. Then you have to react quickly and don't really have time to think. Thus a cross-country skier can be in control of any situation

Practicing in varying snow and track conditions facilitate quick reactions. You gather experiences and develop your reflexes. Now you can probably guess how important It Is to be knowledgeable about your sport. A cross-country skier can decide much quicker what a particular impulse means and how to best respond to it, if he is well prepared and doesn't have to spend a lot of time thinking about it.

TACTICS

You have prepared yourself perfectly, trained well and regularly and your skis are in optimum condition. Now you just need some luck and hopefully the snow and the course layout will work well for you. Was that all? Is there nothing more you can do? Of course there is more you can do!

As an athlete, you together with your trainer, think about the course of preparation, choosing the right material, inspecting the course and planning the competition. You decide whether you will start the race out as fast as possible or "stick" with the skier in front of you. How do you go about passing someone and how do you react at the finish? All of that is called tactics.

You try to use tactical measures to utilize your skiing abilities in the best possible way, thus becoming as fast as possible.

Planning the course of the race

The course is not a regulation-size playing field that you can practice on and ski with your eyes closed. Part of preparing for a cross-country skiing competition definitely includes a close inspection of the course. With your trainer or your teammates, look at the route, the route outline and the elevation profile. You should check the snow conditions and memorize long inclines, the location of treacherous turns and how the run is laid out. With this information you can better plan how to ration your strength, the passing sequences and the final sprint.

Get information about the other starters and the starting order. That is important to better assess their performance and actions and be able to react to them. Choose your skis and wax according to the snow and track conditions and pick weather-appropriate clothing.

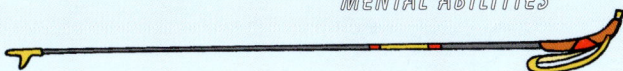

What could your tactics be in the following situations? Write down how you would proceed.

1 *A certain run has a rather sharp turn at the end.*

2 *Another run ends in a slight incline.*

3 *The skier starting after you passes you at a high speed right at the beginning. You know that he always "slumps" at the end because he starts out too fast.*

4 *You want to win today and the strongest skier started just ahead of you.*

5 *You want to make it among the top five and the strongest skier started just behind you.*

WHAT'S GOING ON WITH YOU?

COACH, I'M MENTALLY REVIEWING THE COURSE AND I NEARLY LOST MY BALANCE IN THAT SHARP TURN!

THE MENTAL STATE AFFECTS THE PERFORMANCE

You prepare for a race by training a lot. You continuously work on your fitness level and refine your technique. You get tips, correct mistakes and practice until you've got it. Now you are exceptionally well prepared and should just have to do everything like you do at practice.

But what's going on? You are shaking with anxiety, afraid you'll fail or something will go wrong. You can barely concentrate on the race. Are you now hopelessly at the mercy of your feelings and your trembling legs, or can the psyche be trained, as well? We assure you that there is something you can do!

First of all, it is very important to know exactly what is going on inside of you. When you know the causes of your anxiety, you can adapt yourself more easily and prepare for such situations.

Tension and nervousness

Excitement before a competition is normal and important. No athlete can be successful if he is totally relaxed and laid back about everything. This inner tension helps you to perform at your best. However, too much excitement is bad. You cannot concentrate as well, are stiff and – most importantly – you make mistakes.

Fear

There are different reasons why a cross-country skier may be afraid. Sometimes it is fear of skiing poorly and failing. At a first glance, inclines or steep downhill stretches with a turn can look very difficult and hard to manage. Maybe you even had a painful fall recently. Or are you not sure you chose the right material and wax? Some opponents also ski rather aggressively and you have to counter that. A little fear is very useful. It makes you more serious and vigilant. Other than that a fearful

skier is unsure of himself and lacks the necessary bite. You can combat that negative feeling through training, by talking to your trainer, your parents or friends. Relaxation exercises are often helpful.

Anger

You can be angry at many things – your trainer, your parents, your friend, the opponent, school, etc. Maybe that training or competition run did not go as well as you had planned. Are you sometimes angry at your "awful" skis? You must learn to deal with aggressive feelings. Don't make your trainer or teammate the focus of your anger. If you feel angry, use that feeling to tackle the task at hand with more focus and spirit. Be aggressive, but not unfair! Stay calm and use it as an incentive.

Talking to yourself a little can often help with your concentration, give you courage and spur you on!

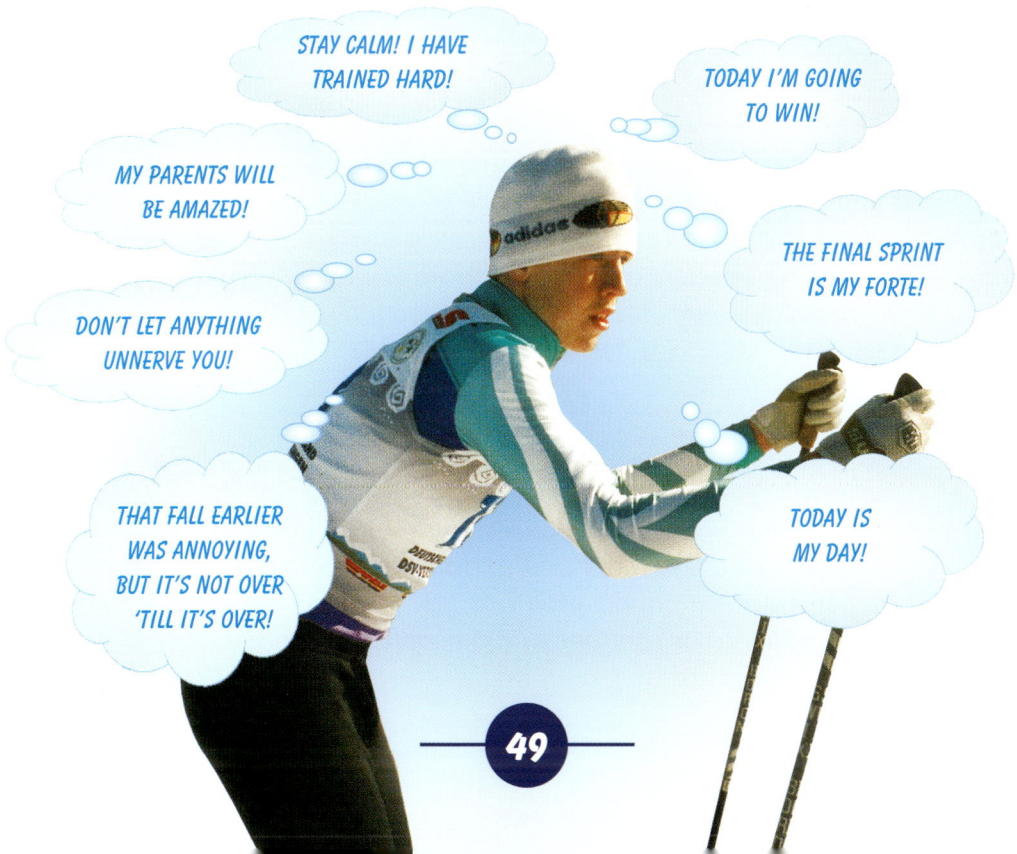

STAY CALM! I HAVE TRAINED HARD!

TODAY I'M GOING TO WIN!

MY PARENTS WILL BE AMAZED!

THE FINAL SPRINT IS MY FORTE!

DON'T LET ANYTHING UNNERVE YOU!

THAT FALL EARLIER WAS ANNOYING, BUT IT'S NOT OVER 'TILL IT'S OVER!

TODAY IS MY DAY!

Perseverance

A cross-country skier will always be in situations where he is excited, afraid or angry, where he pushes himself to the limit or is just plain unenthusiastic. He should be able to tough it out at practice, get better and, when necessary, grit his teeth and bear it. Always look for new challenges and be ready to try something new. You will meet your limits time and again, and learn to push past them in a sensible way.

Such challenges include:

Fear of high speed.
("I will lose control, I will go too fast downhill, I will fall at any moment.")

Limited physical capacity in training.
("I can't go on, it is too strenuous! I can't keep the pace, I am totally exhausted and worn out!")

Fear of new things.
("The way I used to do it always worked so well! I have to get used to the new skis with the new bindings first, surely I'll be slower and less good in competition at first!")

Conflict with trainers or training buddies
("No one understands me! No one notices my difficulties! No one helps me! No one likes me!")

Get over your fears and you will be proud of yourself later. Perseverance in sports toughens you up and also helps you cope with problems at school and in other areas of your life. If you're not sure how to handle problems, get some advice. Your parents, trainer, friends or your doctor are people you can talk to.

Attentiveness and the ability to concentrate

Whether the sun is just coming out from behind the clouds, heavy snow begins to fall or your closest rival shows up at the start with the best ski equipment, don't get distracted! Before a race, the athlete must concentrate completely on his movements and the course. Thinking about private issues, fear of possible mistakes or a poor result is distracting. Problems at school or what to wear to the next party should also be disregarded during practice or competition. The more difficult a task, the more you should concentrate on it. A cross-country skiing competition is very strenuous and you have to gather all of your strength. When your thoughts wander, you will slow down, and just the briefest moment of inattention can cause a fall.

Tips for improving attentiveness

To be attentive, you have to want to be!

When you don't really feel like concentrating on your homework anymore, every little thing will distract you. You think about what your friends are doing, watch a bird fly past the window, and pay attention to every noise in the house. Before you begin to concentrate, tell yourself why you are doing it and what it is good for.

Don't let anything or anyone distract you!

Compare yourself to a spotlight that is directed at one single spot. Only that spot is very bright, everything else is in the dark. Concentrate on the course. Even just looking to see what's going on at the edge of the course can lead to a mistake. Also, thinking about what would happen if you choose the wrong speed will distract you.

Take a concentration break!

Your ability to concentrate is not endless. Every person has to rest and renew his strength.

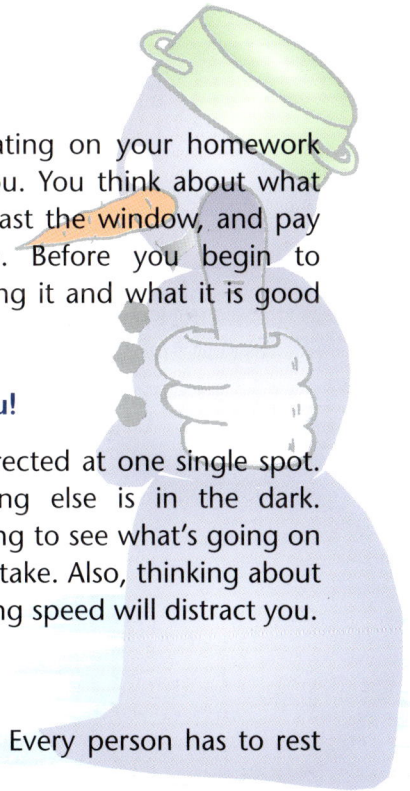

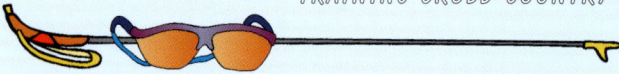

1 **Do you have enough imagination?**

There once was a little bug in love walking along a hair ribbon to get to his sweetheart. Will he make it or will he end up on the wrong side of the ribbon?

2 **How attentive are you?**

Look closely at the photo on page 9 for ten seconds. (Count to ten!) Then come back to this page and try to answer the following questions from memory.

1 Are there two or more skiers shown on the right side?

2 What color is the trainer's hat?

3 Does the skier on the right carry poles?

4 How many skiers are there on the left?

SELF-CONFIDENCE

Some say, "Self-confidence is half the battle!" Of course it isn't quite that simple, but there is some truth to that saying. Someone whose approach is self-confident, who believes in himself and his form certainly has a better chance at success than someone who is afraid and full of doubt.

> HEH, HEH! THAT RACE IS CHILD'S PLAY FOR ME. I AM THE FASTEST AND THE BEST! WHAT ARE YOU CLOWNS DOING HERE ANYWAY?

But you shouldn't get reckless and make a mistake because of too much confidence!

> OH BOY! IT'S NOT GOING TO WORK AGAIN! I'M JUST PLAIN BAD AND I ALWAYS LOSE. WHEN I LOOK AT THE OTHERS, I JUST WANT TO GO HOME.

Which of the following qualities and attitudes can you, as a skier, benefit from, and which are more of a hindrance? Cross out anything you don't want to have too much of.

Self-confidence – joy in cross-country skiing – self-doubt – blind rage – willingness to take risks – impatience – being laid-back – fear of making mistakes – ambition – desire to win – faith in one's performance – pessimism – bad mood – feeling in great form – attentiveness – concentration

Even the best athlete loses sometimes

If you are too slow, don't have enough strength, can't push off properly, make technical mistakes or even fall down, you will wonder where the problem lies. Maybe you weren't in good form, the course was too difficult and the opponents were older than you. They have trained longer and therefore are stronger. Maybe the snow conditions weren't favorable and your skis weren't perfectly prepped. Don't be angry, but keep on practicing. If you're good, you'll do better next time. Be happy about personal bests.

But if you think you should have done better, then think about the reasons and causes. A chart on which you can list the reasons for your poor performance can help you with that.

When I was dissatisfied with my performance...	What were the reasons?	What do I want to do in the near future?
The others were much faster on the downhill.	The gliding quality of the skis was limited / not optimal.	Prepare skis better and familiarize myself better with course profile.
Not enough strength endurance in the arms.	My arm action was too weak.	Increase strength endurance training for arms.

SELF-IMPOSED PRESSURE BUILDS MENTAL STRENGTH

What do you think about this story about Julie? Does it sound familiar?

Julie has been looking forward to the competition. She has told everyone how well things are going at practice, and that the trainer has signed her up for the next competition. She was well prepared. She packed her bag the night before and checked off everything on her checklist. Now it's early to bed to get rested up for the big day! But then several skiers pass her in the race and she even falls down in a shallow turn. Everyone is surprised and wonders what is going on with Julie today.

What happened to Julie is something that can happen even to very successful athletes during important races.

The pressure was too much; she was too excited and could not give her usual performance. But that isn't the end of a career, although it is very annoying!

You should know why such a situation occurs and what you can do about it.

PRESSURE AFFECTS YOUR EXPECTATIONS

On the one hand, there are external expectations. They come from your parents, your trainer and your friends. They all expect you to perform well.

BRAVO, YOU ARE THE BEST!
WE'RE PROUD OF YOU!
TODAY YOU WILL WIN!
SHOW THEM WHAT YOU CAN DO!
I'M COUNTING ON YOU!

I WANT TO WIN TODAY!
I'M GOING TO SHOW THEM!
I'M GOING TO SKI FAST!
EVERYONE WILL BE PROUD AND CHEER!
ALL THAT TRAINING IS WORTH IT!

And then add to that your own expectations. You want to reach the goals you set for yourself.

Sometimes the pressure of these expectations is too much. You become afraid of not being able to meet the expectations that others or you yourself have of you. And that's stressful!

How to deal with pressure

Get well prepared for the competition during the week at practice. Train diligently and with concentration. Prepare yourself properly for the demands that await you. Then nothing that happens will be a surprise.

Get everything ready the night before, check your equipment, go to bed early, eat a good breakfast and leave your house on time.

Leave behind any problems that have nothing to do with the competition. Imagine that no other problems can touch you once you're on the track. Only concentrate on your movements and the course.

You chose the pressure yourself. You set the goals and determine what you want to achieve. Of course, you could also set goals that are easier to reach and avoid the pressure by skiing slower, not wanting to win anyway, or by not even starting at all. Set high but realistic goals for yourself. A little pressure is necessary. It's fun, spurs you on and gets you moving.

Pressure builds character! You will only get strong if you can handle pressure situations. Each time, you will be able to handle more pressure. Someone who already avoids pressure in the preparation phase will become a "weakling," and will always fall short of his potential. Conquering your fears will strengthen your character.

Watch successful athletes as they relax and concentrate before a race, at the start and during breaks. How do they react to mistakes, a situation change in the competition, successes and defeats? Try to emulate them and find out what works best for you. Practice these rituals and carry them out again and again. Character traits you develop through skiing will also be useful in other areas of life!

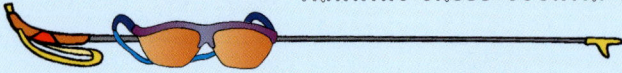

TEST

How would you react in the following situations?

1. Situation: You don't feel like going to practice.

A Of course you stay at home because you shouldn't force yourself. **1**

B You go to practice without much enthusiasm because you don't want to disappoint your parents. **2**

C You go to practice like you always do because missing practice will make you get bad again. Maybe you will feel like practicing once you get on your skis. **3**

2. Situation: The trainer repeatedly criticizes your skating technique.

A It is irritating that it doesn't work very well yet. But first you are going to work on using your poles properly. **2**

B He shouldn't be so petty all the time. It's not a beauty contest. One more word and you're leaving! **1**

C It's good that the trainer is always watching. That way certain mistakes won't be able to creep in at all. **3**

3. Situation: The race course looks pretty tough.

A You are totally focused, your breathing is calm and you mentally go over the difficult sections one more time. **3**

B You think you can easily do it. You take another look to see if all your relatives are there, and wave to them. **2**

C You are afraid you'll "mess up" the whole thing. You have already decided that you will lose too much time on the incline. You don't have a chance against the others anyway. **1**

4. Situation: Last week the trainer told you that Tom will be on the relay team instead of you.

A   You think, too bad, maybe I just wasn't good enough.   **2**

B   You are upset because you are at least as good as Tom. Hopefully, he won't do well and I can say: "I would have been faster!"   **1**

C   You help Tom and support him in everything he needs. You work hard during practice so you will be chosen next time.   **3**

5. Situation: At the left fork you go straight, losing precious time.

A   It makes perfect sense. The turn-off was not properly marked.   **1**

B   That can happen. But now I'm back in my ski rhythm, and I'll make up the time.   **3**

C   Going the wrong way is just that. The others will make their jokes, but I'll finish the race as best I can.   **2**

6. Situation: You see another skier secretly tampering with the favorite's ski.

A   You confront him and demand that he immediately fix it.   **3**

B   You decide to wait. It's not your problem; one shouldn't get involved in everything.   **2**

C   Great idea! If the overall favorite is out of the picture, you, too, have a good chance of winning.   **1**

Add up your points! You will find what your score means in the solutions section on page 144.

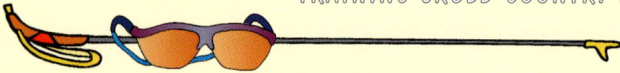

RELAXATION EXERCISES

To relax, find a quiet spot where no one will disturb you. Sit or lie down, or lean against a wall and close your eyes. The most important part is breathing properly.

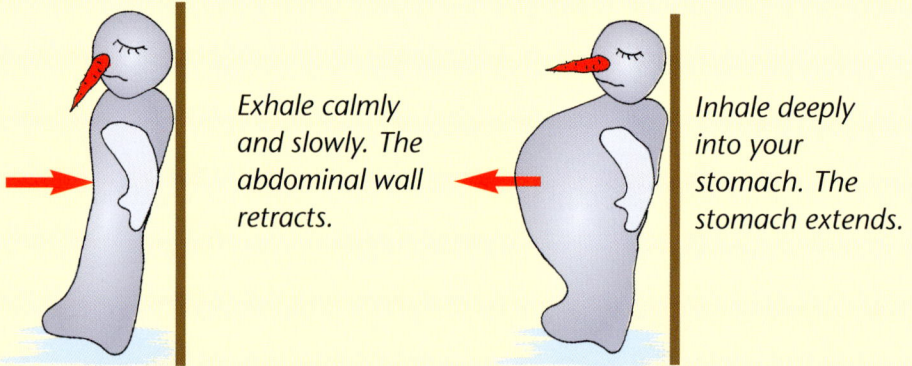

Exhale calmly and slowly. The abdominal wall retracts.

Inhale deeply into your stomach. The stomach extends.

The following exercises will stretch your muscles and tendons. You will feel a slight pulling. That 's good, but it shouldn't hurt. Hold the position as long as you comfortably can. No bouncing! Don't forget that good belly breathing when doing the following exercises! You can find more exercises in, for instance, yoga books.

Make yourself really small like a little package.

Get on your back and extend your legs back over your head.

From a kneeling position, rock back on your heels and then lean really far forward.

. . . . 6 PHYSICAL FITNESS

Max visits the doctor because he thinks that something is not quite right with his body. "I don't know what's wrong with me. Yesterday we practiced in the new ski stadium. I was totally exhausted, and at the end, I was barely able to stay on my feet. Also, my upper arms hurt and my legs were cramping!"

"You most likely didn't train enough!"
"But I go to practice three times a week. There I practice double poling and gliding correctly on two legs and on one leg."
"And what else do you do for training?"
"What do you mean? I'm skiing the entire time!"

What will the doctor tell Max? His training is too one-sided. He forgot about fitness training. He has no endurance, no strength, and his joints are not flexible. His body cannot handle the regular training with intense load-bearing phases.

WHAT PHYSICAL FITNESS MEANS

In sports the term physical fitness refers primarily to physical abilities. Your fitness level determines how much endurance and speed you have, how strong you are and how much physical strain you can handle. You can tell whether your fitness level is good or not by, for instance, how quickly you get winded after a short race, how long you can bear up under athletic strain without all of your limbs hurting, or how quickly you get tired.

You get physically fit through regular training on the course. But you can also get fit and improve your fitness by engaging in many other supplementary sports.

S	W	I	M	M	I	N	G	T	M	O	P	L	X	H
H	F	C	R	O	S	S	C	O	U	N	T	R	Y	G
I	G	E	L	R	U	I	M	W	S	I	N	N	E	T
K	N	S	F	E	S	N	O	T	N	I	M	D	A	B
I	I	K	F	P	T	G	N	I	L	C	Y	C	I	B
N	E	A	X	E	R	E	C	C	O	S	Z	W	B	U
G	O	T	V	L	X	S	N	I	U	K	P	U	T	E
X	N	I	H	L	Z	R	Y	R	T	N	C	P	M	W
J	A	N	R	I	G	K	F	M	I	W	Z	Q	N	X
H	C	G	M	N	W	I	L	L	A	B	D	N	A	H
J	U	D	O	G	N	J	O	G	G	I	N	G	B	X
N	V	S	O	G	Y	M	N	A	S	T	I	C	S	L
T	Y	B	Y	W	L	L	A	B	Y	E	L	L	O	V
B	I	G	N	I	T	A	K	S	E	N	I	L	N	I

Some sports you can do alone and others you can only do with a team. There are also typical summer and winter sports. In this puzzle, we have hidden 16 of these sports horizontally, vertically, forward, backward and diagonally. Can you find them?

FITNESS-RELATED ABILITIES

We will now take a closer look at the most important fitness-related abilities a cross-country skier must have to be in all-around good shape. They include:

Endurance

Strength

Speed

Endurance

Endurance is the fitness-related ability one needs to handle long-term physical strain. Since cross-country skiing is primarily an endurance sport, endurance is a very important component. That also includes not getting tired quickly from strenuous training, a long competition day, or during long trips to competitions. Your body should also be able to recover quickly after great physical strain. That is called regeneration. When someone has good endurance, he is physically fit, recovers quicker after practice and competition, and is able to concentrate longer. Endurance training is particularly important in skiing. We differentiate between general endurance training (jogging, biking, swimming, game sports, track and field, etc.) and special endurance training (cross-country skiing and roller skiing for more than an hour), as well as forms of endurance training with additional resistance (strength endurance training) or very high intensity (speed endurance training).

How can you train for endurance?

Special endurance training is done with roller skis or cross-country skis under the direction of the trainer. But aside from training at the club, there are many other opportunities and possibilities during the course

of the year for you to train specifically for general endurance (basic endurance). In summer, the cross-country skier trains with roller skis, Nordic inline skating, cross-country running and mountain biking. Of course, in winter you log many miles on the track with cross-country skis.

Many other sports are also suitable for improving and increasing your endurance, such as swimming, biking, paddling, and many more. Any ball sport that requires a lot of running, such as handball, soccer, hockey, tennis, etc., also offers great endurance training.

Speed

Speed is the ability you need to execute a movement with the most acceleration and speed possible. Critical here is the fastest possible muscle response (contraction of muscles). Of particular importance for a cross-country skier is speed endurance. It is necessary for increasing speed and when you want to accelerate as you sprint down the home stretch. You need movement speed, meaning a quick implementation of technique, and reaction speed to be able to react quick as a flash in a new situation.

How can you train for speed?

Here, too, the same rule applies: The best speed training is done on skis. So don't do your training in slow motion, but practice at full speed as soon as you have mastered the motion sequence. Outside the cross-country course, any ball games in which you have to move fast and react very quickly are well suited. But you can also train for speed by sprinting (even on a bike), by jumping rope quickly, or with reaction games

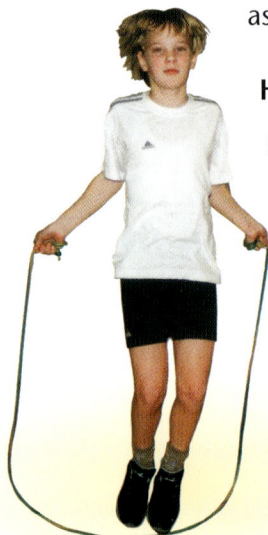

like those we described in chapter 5, "Mental Abilities." Make sure the sprinting distance or time period of increased speed you choose for speed endurance training is not too short.

Strength

Strength is necessary for moving something heavy, like lifting, pushing, pulling or pressing weights. Without strength it is not possible to execute movements, particularly athletic movements.

You also need strength to hold your body or parts of your body in a certain position, to move them as fast as possible or to slow down a movement. As a cross-country skier ,you need lots of arm strength for powerful poling. You also need a lot of leg strength to push off forcefully, to manage the incline and the turn.

How can you train for strength?

Surely you have seen the many machines fitness studios have for athletes to steel their muscles on. Actually, you don't really need any elaborate "strength machines," but with some simple weights and your own body, you can get in shape quite well. In summer, take advantage of possible mountain hiking, mountain running, mountain biking or stair training.

TEST REQUIREMENTS FOR YOUNG CROSS-COUNTRY SKIERS

Test		Personal Performance	Goal
Long distance: Summer: 1,000–3, 000 m	Time:		
Winter: 3–10 km roller ski or ski	Time:		
Sprint: 15 m flying start	Time:		
Stride jumps In 30 m, flying start	Min. no.:		
Push-ups	Max. no.:		
Jump up and reach Number in 30 sec.	Max. no.:		
Knee bends Number in 1 min.	Max. no.:		
Triple jump (Stand.-left-right-final jump)	Dist:		
Long jump (final) From standing position	Dist.:		

Here you can record your results. It is best to use a pencil so you can always update your current best. Also track your performance development as you do the exercises.

WARMING UP – STRETCHING – LIMBERING UP

Regardless of whether you are starting with cross-country training or supplementary fitness training, want to do exercises at home or are at a competition – this rule always applies! It is important that you prepare your body for the impending strain.

At the end of the school day or after a rest, your muscles are still relatively cold and stiff, and your breathing is still on "normal mode." Gradually, everything is prepared for training and competition. Once things get started, your "engine will already be warm" and you can perform purposefully and easily.

Warming up

As the word suggests, you are getting warm! A variety of exercises help to get your muscles activated, improve their circulation and get them ready to perform. An indication for this is limberness, flexibility, a slight reddening of the skin and perspiration. It is a way to prevent injuries such as strains.

Any movement that gets you going is good for warming up:

Jogging, easy jumps, calisthenics, ball games – even some light skiing and easy downhill stretches.

WHAT'S THIS?

BUT COACH, WE WERE SUPPOSED TO WARM UP!

All training sessions begin with the warm-up. That also goes for doing exercises at home, before a race, or when you are late for practice. You can jog a few laps, do some jumps or jump rope by yourself.

Stretching muscles

Flexibility is increased primarily by stretching the muscles. You cannot just strengthen one muscle alone, but always have to keep in mind the antagonist, the "opposing player."

The illustration shows the "muscle man" with a bent arm. Responsible for this bending is the flexor, the **biceps**. That is the muscle that contracts when you want to show someone "your muscles." The extensor, the **triceps,** is responsible for the extension of the arm.

Feel your muscles! Try the following exercise:
If you push down on a tabletop with your hand, the triceps gets hard because it wants to extend the arm in the elbow. The biceps is soft because it is relaxed and yields. But if you push against the table from below, the biceps is hard and the triceps is soft. That's how it should be.

The cross-country skiers are stretching their leg muscles.

Limbering up

Although you have warmed up and stretched sufficiently, the muscles are often stiff and tense after a strenuous practice. After you have finished stretching, it is important to loosen up.

Most of the time you do these exercises automatically. You shake out your arms, legs and hands and move your joints gently in all directions. Easy jogging or jumping can also help you loosen up.

> WHAT'S GOING ON WITH YOU?

> OH, COACH! I GUESS I DID TOO MANY LIMBERING EXERCISES. I FEEL SO LOOSE ...!

This preparation time does not only get your muscles warmed up and your entire body moving, but your head is also adjusting to the impending strain.

In doing so, you shake off all worries and problems, and feel free and ready to take on whatever will come.

When stretching out, you stretch the muscle group you just worked. Here are a few stretching exercises. Can you feel your muscles? Have fun!

STRETCHING THE
GLUTEAL MUSCLES.

STRETCHING THE INNER
THIGH.

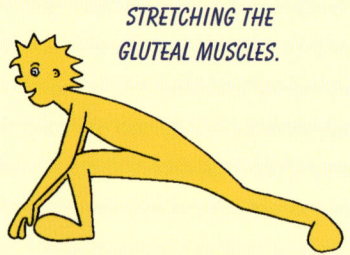

STRETCHING THE
FRONT OF THE
THIGH.

STRETCHING THE BACK
OF THE THIGH.

STRETCHING
THE HAMSTRING.

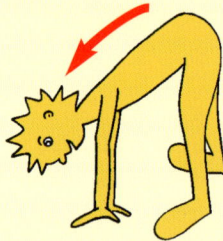

STRETCHING THE OBLIQUE
TRUNK MUSCLES.

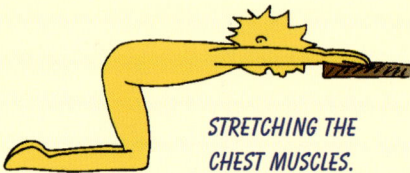

STRETCHING THE
CHEST MUSCLES.

STRETCHING THE LOWER BACK.

Count to 20 as you hold each stretch, loosen up the muscles and then stretch again. Remember: The exercises are meant to stretch the muscles; they should not hurt!

.... 7 COORDINATION

What the snowman is doing here is fantastic. He is balancing on Skitty's head with one hand and waving with the other hand. At the same time he is balancing the pot and pieces of coal on his feet and singing a song.

Many muscles are used for such an acrobatic feat and all of the movements are coordinated. He has to keep his balance while waving in a rhythm; he can't lose the objects and of course has to remember the words to his song. In addition he should always keep an eye on Skitty in case he suddenly moves. And what happens if there is a sudden gust of wind?

The cross-country skier skis uphill and downhill in constantly changing terrain, in variable snow conditions under increasing fatigue. At the same time, he has to constantly keep an eye on the opponent and the competitive situation.

Being able to properly handle these demands, as well as finding the correct rhythm and keeping your balance, requires *coordinative abilities*. These are very specific abilities that you, as a cross-country skier, have to develop. All movements are precisely coordinated and adapted to the situation on the course.

In this chapter, we would like to more closely define the important coordinative abilities a cross-country skier depends on.

Linking ability

As the word suggests, movements are linked, meaning they are connected to each other. The leg movement with pushing off and gliding, as well as the pole application, is coordinated.

Orientation ability

When the skier is on the course, a good sense of orientation is very important. The circumstances on the course are constantly changing. There are inclines, downhill stretches and directional changes. You have to adjust your skiing accordingly and accurately calculate speed, gradient and distances. That allows you to react ideally in every situation.

Adaptability and adjustability

In cross-country skiing, the situation changes constantly. You continuously have to adjust to new circumstances on the course and adapt your ski technique. But sometimes there are also unexpected situations: You slide, touch the barrier, there is something on the track, you have trouble keeping your balance or your skis are poorly prepped. With this huge physical exertion, you hardly have time to think, but must quickly adjust to the new situation and sometimes even deviate from your plan.

Balance

It is rather difficult to stand upright on a bar. You keep your balance by tensing your muscles and making small balancing movements. The skier tries to always maintain his balance over the narrow ski. Add to that the fact that the cross-country skier is continuously moving, always has a different body position and therefore has to constantly find the ideal position over the ski.

In addition, there are the changing snow conditions, varying gradients, inclines, bumps, turns, wind, etc.

This is how you can train for balance!

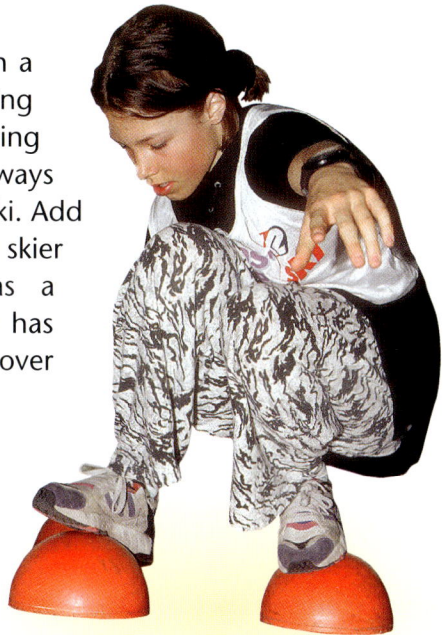

Someone who trains regularly becomes increasingly confident and more and more comfortable with balancing on a ski. At the same time, you also learn to always find your balance in different course conditions. Without snow, you can practice with inline skates or do special gymnastics exercises.

Rhythmic ability

In cross-country skiing, there are movements that always repeat themselves in a certain sequence: Push off – poles – glide. This is called a cycle. When this cycle is performed nice and evenly, the rhythm can be recognized. Many recreational athletes love the feeling of skiing in a regular rhythm: One – two – one – two – etc. This is hardly possible in a competition. Inclines, downhill stretches, turns, passing maneuvers or the final sprint constantly require technique, and thereby force you to change your rhythm and adapt it to the conditions.

Motor reaction ability

As bicyclists and drivers already know from street traffic: The higher your speed, the quicker the reaction to an unexpected event must be. In a competition you sometimes move at a pretty high speed and it is therefore important to be able to react quickly to an unforeseen situation. If you suddenly slip, are hindered by another skier or a spectator, or are almost carried out of a turn, you have to react immediately.

MUSCLE SENSE

Parents and teachers often talk about the **five senses** you should use when you want to learn something new. What they are trying to say is that you should listen well, watch carefully, touch the surface, smell it and taste it. Surely you have noticed that not all senses are always used equally.

SEEING

HEARING BALANCE

TOUCHING

TASTING

SMELLING

Senses that are important in skiing

You certainly can't taste anything when you ski. Smelling is more of a secondary effect when you get a whiff of that fresh winter air or you are in the wax room. That you need to see to ski doesn't require an explanation. But during a competition you also have to be able to hear: the rhythm of movement, the snow and the cheering of the spectators. Part of the organ called the ear is also your sense of balance. You need that so you don't lose your balance and fall despite the fast movements.

Some people even talk about a sixth sense. Cross-country skiers need such a sixth sense for the muscle sense or sense of movement. We will simply call it **"muscle sense."** It is very important for learning and mastering technique in cross-country skiing. During a race, the skier looks at the course, the snow conditions and his competitors. He can't look at how his skis are positioned or whether or not he is using the poles properly. He must be able to "feel" these things. And this "feeling" or "muscle sense," is developed by practicing diligently in training.

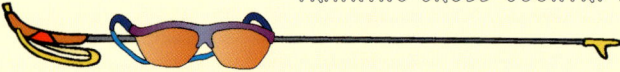

DEXTERITY EXERCISES

There are many exercises to help you move around safely and skillfully on those "skinny boards." Here we will only show you a small selection. Your trainer will surely have many more ideas.

On the plain

• Tromping, climbing, jumping, step-turning, turning around
• Relay games, racing, playing catch, obstacle course
• Dodge ball, soccer, handball

Going downhill

• Snow plow, breaking, schussing
• Skiing through gates, skiing through low gates, skiing slalom
• Jumping while skiing, step-turning, squatting

Do lots of exercises without poles!

8 TECHNIQUE

Have you ever tried to juggle five bowling pins or balls? Some acrobats use burning torches or sharp knives, balancing them as they ride on a bicycle. Even the best acrobats were not able to do that when they were babies.

To master skills like these, one has to practice long and hard until one has mastered them perfectly. A good skier must master the skiing technique just as well. Most often it is a combination of many small movements that make up a certain technique.

You have already learned the most important movements on skis, such as walking and gliding on flat terrain, going up an incline or down a hill, during your initial years as a skier.

During continued training new ones will be added to these. In doing so, you will continue to refine the classic technique and the skating. You practice different options for skiing turns and how to handle an incline. You try different ways of using the poles and adapt them to the arm and leg rhythm. This is the way you will continue to practice the transition from one technique to another.

In a competition, the movements have to be automatic!

If a competition requires all of your strength, you are exhausted and reaching your capacity, you won't be

able to think about which leg pushes off first, which leg will glide and where the poles have to be applied. That must all happen automatically.

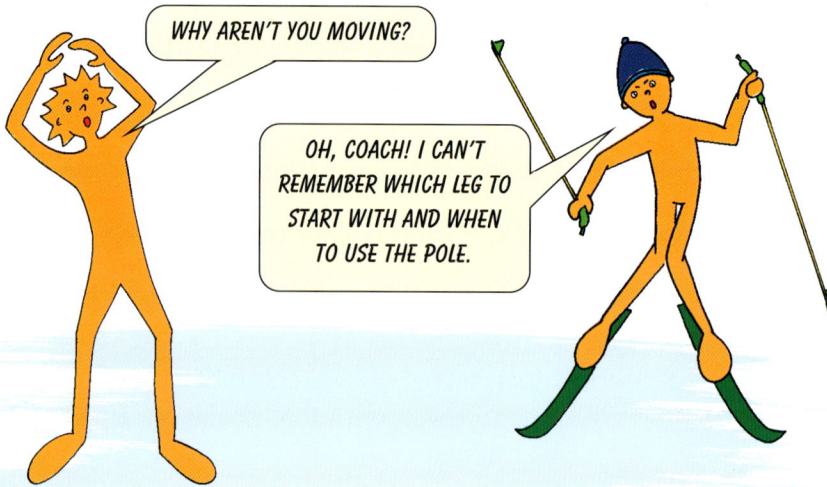

WHY AREN'T YOU MOVING?

OH, COACH! I CAN'T REMEMBER WHICH LEG TO START WITH AND WHEN TO USE THE POLE.

The technique must be practiced until it works perfectly. In training, you will practice the techniques and motion sequences again and again in many different ways, until you no longer have to think about every single step.

TECHNIQUE TRAINING

When you learn a new technique, it is usually introduced via an explanation and a demonstration by the trainer or ski instructor. They explain the motion sequence, tell you what you have to pay particular attention to and what mistakes to avoid.

Just like in school, there are different methods for learning. As people are different, they also have different ways of learning or memorizing something new. The trainer will work with the different learning types

and introduce new material through a variety of methods. Often it is a combination of different ways of learning that is successful.

These include:

❄ The trainer explains the new technique.
❄ The trainer or another skier demonstrates the technique.
❄ The new technique is shown via drawings or sequence pictures.
❄ Possible mistakes are discussed with the aid of error images.
❄ Videos are shown.
❄ The trainer asks the athletes to describe and explain the new technique.
❄ The athletes make sketches.
❄ They try the new technique themselves.
❄ The technique is executed with monitoring and suggestions by the trainer.
❄ The technique is executed with monitoring and suggestions by training buddies.
❄ The athletes do dry exercises without skis.

What learning type are you? Check the learning methods that are most helpful to you when learning a new technique. Try out what works best for you!

Perseverance brings success

After the trainer's explanation and demonstration, it is your turn to practice the new material. Of course, it is lots of fun to learn and execute a new technique. In the beginning, the movements tend to be fairly loose, and you are just trying to make sure that your arms and legs are doing it right. You quickly see some progress. Your movements become surer and faster. Your trainer will notice, too. He will surely compliment you and that will spur you on to continue practicing and getting better and better. But gradually all that practicing gets dull. You don't notice an obvious improvement of your performance anymore and the thrill of something new is gone as well. You are thinking that

things are already going pretty well with this new technique. Why keep practicing? Now comes the point when you may not feel like doing it anymore. But if you quit now, you will forget some things and all that practicing before will be for nothing. So remember what you have resolved to do and fight your "inner couch potato"!

THE ROAD TO INCREASED PERFORMANCE

After that quick progress there will be many training days when you will feel like nothing is happening. It is important to know that this stage will come. On the long road to perfect technique there are always stages of quick progress, and also stages of grinding drudgery. So if you think it can't get any better and you have already reached your performance capacity and any further practice seems useless, keep on trying and you will see that it does get better.

During this apparent standstill, your body is preparing for the next level of performance development. You could say it is getting internally programmed for the next step. That sometimes happens overnight.

So don't let an apparent standstill drive you to despair. These are necessary transitional phases. The key is perseverance! Your trainer knows that, too, and will let you keep on practicing.

Some techniques you will learn relatively quickly. Others require many, many hours of training, even years. Rest assured – persistent and arduous training pays off!

Tips for training technique

- Listen and watch closely when the technique is being explained, shown through pictures, and demonstrated.

- Mentally retrace the technique and, with your eyes closed, concentrate on visualizing the sequence and the movement.

- Practice the technique over and over again in training. Monitor yourself after every repetition or have others observe what needs improvement.

- Take your time looking over the illustrations one more time, going through the descriptions and comparing them to your movements. It helps to explain, describe and show the technique to someone else.

- Monitor and help each other!

- In training, try to practice in varying snow and course conditions and with different materials.

How a cross-country skier practices to perfect a new technique is just like learning at school – different for everyone. However, everyone has to practice a lot. In the end, the technique should be executed accurately and without progress monitoring, meaning *automatically*.

The progressions are "programmed" and stored in your brain through the many repetitions. It is almost like downloading a computer program that will later be accessed again.

If you don't work hard in training, are skiing unfocused and sloppy, the wrong sequences will be stored. When something incorrect has been memorized it will take a lot of effort to break that habit again later.

MONITORING – EVALUATING – IMPROVING

Don't learn anything incorrect and automate it! That is why you need to monitor the progression of a new technique, recognize the mistakes and execute the movement increasingly faster and more accurately. How quickly that works also depends on your *goals* and your *motivation*. Do you remember Julie?

The trainer practiced step turns with the training group and now everyone can demonstrate on an unfamiliar run with a turn. Julie tries very hard. The trainer watches her and says, "Great, Julie! You are doing well!" Julie is happy and keeps practicing.

Several training sessions later the trainer is again watching and says, "That's not so great yet, Julie. You are not shifting your weight and you are losing too much speed!" Now Julie is upset. She skied the turn the same way she did several days ago. Then, the trainer complimented her and now he is nagging!

As you have probably already noticed, the trainer in this story did not make a mistake. He only adapted his evaluation to the situation and the potential outcomes. Julie's step turns were certainly not perfect in the beginning. But they were pretty good for a first time. But later, after many repetitions, an improvement should be expected. The next sub-goal should be reached.

You reach many sub-goals on the road to perfect technique, and every little mistake is observed and corrected. Evaluation by the trainer is best since he knows the most about skiing.

. . . . 9 TRAINING PLAN

Someone who regularly trains in cross-country skiing wants to go to competitions and match himself with others and win. That is why it is so important that your training be systematic and geared to a specific goal.

When you pack your bags for vacation, you have to know whether you are going to the mountains or to the ocean. And when you write a letter, you should first determine who you are sending it to.

Therefore it is very important for the competitive athlete to gear his training to a big competition. On that day you want to be in top form, at the peak of your capacity.

You build yourself up during training: You strengthen your muscles, improve your endurance, strengthen your lungs for sufficient oxygen intake, refine your technique, and mentally you are in top form.

But in the course of the training year you will also experience physical lows. You will feel weak, drained, without strength, and won't feel like doing anything. That is normal, but it should definitely not happen on the day of a competition!

That is why you absolutely have to establish a yearly training plan!

THE YEARLY PLAN

If athletes in endurance sports such as swimming, biking, running, triathlon, and of course cross-country skiing, want to improve their performance, they must train year-round. A well-structured training program in appropriate training segments is crucial to success.

Dividing the training year into three fundamental phases has proven successful. It could look something like this:

Preparation period, phase 1
20th to 33rd calendar week (approx. mid-May to mid-August)

During this time, strength endurance and a general performance basics are developed with minimal load intensity. The number and scope of the training units slowly increases. The training content can consist of jogging, strength training, paddling, rowing, biking, mountain biking, inline skating or roller skiing.

Preparation period, phase 2
34th to 44th calendar week (approx. mid-August to October)

Increase of basic and strength endurance should continue based on the achieved performance increase. Higher speed ranges are targeted in the course of the performance increase. Twice a week, the level of exertion should be quite high. Specific performance basics are now being developed.

Preparation period, phase 3
45th to 51st calendar week (approx. November to late December)

Now the competition-specific performance basics are being developed. This is the time with the highest training volume of the year. This means high training volume, increased competition-like training and competition-like speed. Now emphasis is also placed on specific technique training on snow. During this time period, the physical load is high to partly very high.

Competition period
52nd to 13th calendar week (approx. late December to March)

Now you must develop your peak athletic form and maintain it for several weeks. During this period, you also have to schedule time for maintaining your basic endurance. The load intensity of training is determined by competitive peaks and particularly by the best-possible structuring of recovery and regeneration phases after competitions. You have to be careful not to reduce your basic endurance with competition-specific training that is too intensive and with too many competitions spaced too close together, thus becoming totally spent. Nevertheless: Look forward to the competitions; they are your best training!

Transition period

At some point you have to step back from the stress of competing and gain motivation, strength and endurance for the next training year. Now it is time to actively recuperate for complete mental and physical regeneration. Participate in other sports you like, get together with your friends, read books and update your training diary. Enjoy the spring and still watch your weight!

Be smart about rationing your strength and get well prepared for the peak of the season!

YEAR-ROUND WEEKLY PLAN

Your ski association can give cross-country skiers recommendations for a year-round weekly plan. It is developed specifically for various age groups. On this page, you can see a year-round weekly plan for **13-year-olds**.

Preparation period, phase 1

Week number	20	21	22	23	24	25	26	27	28	29	30	31	32	33
Roll. ski free tech./km							10	10	10	12	12	13	15	15
Roll. ski class. t./km							10	10	10	12	12	10	12	12
Running/km	12	14	13	16	18	19	19	16	15	16	16	13	15	15
Mnt. Bike/hours	2	2	2	2	2	2	2	2	2	2	2	2	2	2
Total kilometers	12	14	13	16	18	19	39	36	35	40	40	36	42	42
Total t. hours	3:50	4:10	4:00	4:25	4:35	4:45	7:15	6:50	6:40	7:40	7:40	7:20	7:30	7:30
Strength training/hrs.	1		1		1		1	1		1	1		1	
Running on hills/hrs.						2							3	

Preparation period, phase 2

Week number	34	35	36	37	38	39	40	41	42	43	44
Roll. ski free tech./km	15	15	14	14	12	12	15	17	18	20	20
Roll. ski class. t./km	13	13	16	16	16	16	20	20	20	20	20
Running/km	15	15	13	13	13	13	13	12	12	12	12
Mnt. Bike/hours	2	2									
Total kilometers	43	43	43	43	41	41	48	49	50	52	52
Total t. hours	7:10	7:10	5:35	5:35	5:20	5:20	6:10	6:15	6:20	6:30	6:30
Strength training/hrs.	1	1		1	1	1		1	1		1
Running on hills/hrs.					2			2		1	

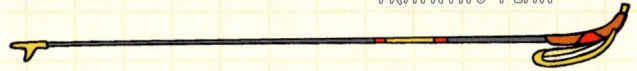

Preparation period, phase 3

Week number	45	46	47	48	49	50	51
Ski free tech./km			15	20	18	20	28
Ski class. tech./km			15	20	25	20	25
Roll. Ski fr. Tech/km	18	18					
Roll. Ski class. t./km	20	20	18	18			
Running/km	8	8	7	8	7	8	7
Total kilometers	46	46	55	64	50	48	60
Total t. hours	5.40	5:40	6:55	8:05	6:25	5:50	7:20
Strength training/hrs.		1		1		1	

Competition period

Week number	52	1	2	3	4	5	6	7	8	9	10	11	12	13
Ski free tech./km	28	30	25	18	18	20	18	20	17	17	17	17	17	17
Ski class. tech./km	30	30	25	20	18	17	20	20	20	20	22	22	22	22
Running/km	8		5	5	5		5		5		5		5	
Total kilometers	64	60	55	43	41	35	45	38	45	37	44	39	44	39
Total t. hours	8:20	7:15	6:50	5:15	6:00	4:05	4:00	4:00	5:25	4:40	5:30	4:50	5:25	4:50
Strength training/hrs.	1		1		1		1		1		1		1	

You should also allow time for approximately 15 minutes of **calisthenics** per day and 1 to 1 1/2 hours of **swimming or games** per week. All roller ski and ski training also includes technique training.

The phase of specific **competition preparation** lasts about 2 to 3 weeks. It begins with a multi-day (active) recuperation. During that time, general training and fitness training are part of the program. After that, the build-up phase begins, during which you adapt your physical capacity to the competition requirements. The week **after the competition** must be structured in such a way that allows you to quickly recover.

SUPERCOMPENSATION

In their research, scientists have figured out how an athlete achieves a performance increase through regular and increasing training.

The graph

The orange line shows the athlete's performance level. In the beginning, in the orange field, it remains constant. During training (blue field), the athlete fatigues with an increasing workload. Then he has to recover (yellow field). During the recovery phase (regeneration), he once again reaches his original capacity and maybe even a little more. In sports, this phase is called supercompensation (red arc).

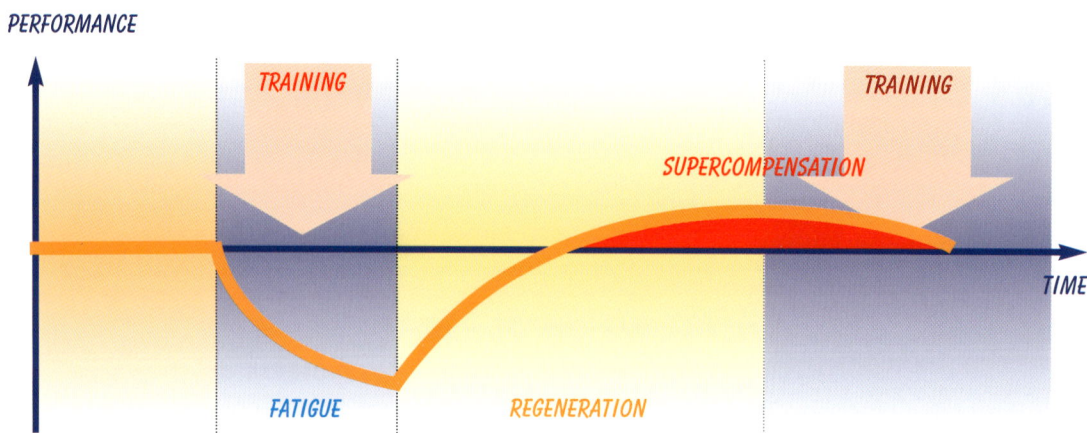

PERFORMANCE

TRAINING

TRAINING

SUPERCOMPENSATION

TIME

FATIGUE

REGENERATION

Relevance to the training plan

If you now take an extended break from training, your performance will return to the old level. That is why it is important that the next training unit happens before the performance curve goes down again.

At some point, your body gets used to the always-recurring workload, plateaus at a certain level and, despite the usual training, no additional performance increase will take place. Now the time has come to increase the training stimulus, meaning the workload. When someone doesn't increase his training, he will get stuck at his old performance level.

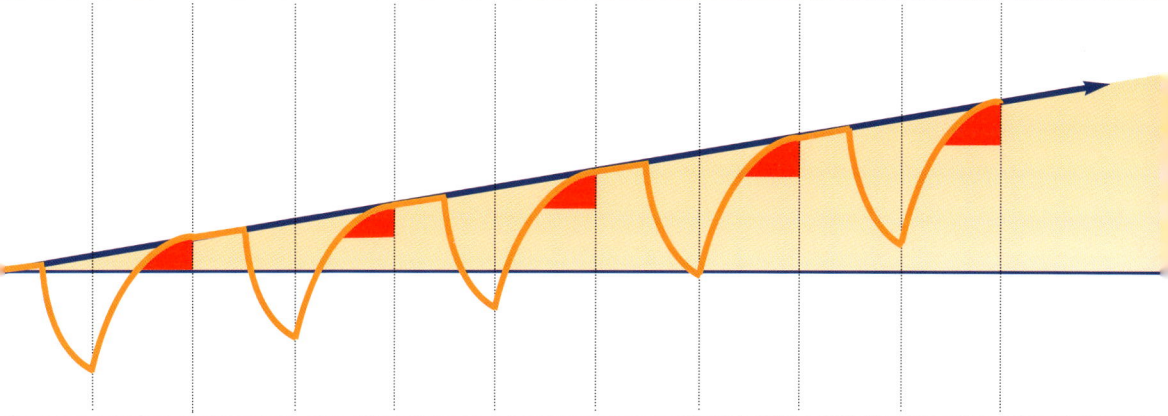

The correct workload

Now it is important that every athlete knows himself and is able to "listen inside himself." If you are in good shape, you recover more quickly. Supercompensation takes place more rapidly, and you can go on with an increased training stimulus.

But if your body is not sufficiently regenerated, the opposite happens. You experience complete exhaustion and decreased performance. If the athlete sets the next training stimulus before complete regeneration, it will cause *overtraining* with a drop in performance and health problems.

Beginners feel their performance increase very quickly. With very fit skiers, it does not happen that rapidly anymore. It takes patience! Also keep in mind that physical factors, like growing, stress, recovering from an illness or injury all affect performance increase.

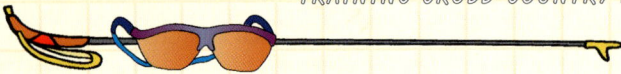

PERFORMANCE GRAPH

Your training results, as well as all competition results, can be shown in a graph. Perhaps you are familiar with this type of illustration from math or physics class. If you can't figure it out right away, ask someone to help you. It's even better if you do it together with your training group.

Take some graph paper and draw graphs. The graduation for axis x can also be done in weeks or months. The graduation for axis y depends on the discipline you are recording; for instance, seconds for sprinting or minutes for jogging, as well as the number of repetitions.

Number

Number of Sit-ups

40	
35	
30	
25	
20	
15	
10	
5	

Jan Feb Mar Apr May Jun Jul Aug Sept Oct Year

200 _

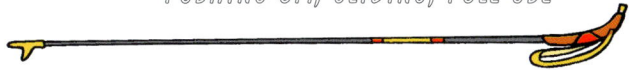

. . . . 10 PUSHING OFF, GLIDING, POLE USE

In the past twenty years, some very important changes have taken place in the sport of cross-country skiing. Due to improved training methods, the skiers continue to increase their physical capacity all the time, and the ski material, the wax and the waxing techniques, as well as the preparation of competition sites are constantly changing. This has continuously advanced the evolution of cross-country skiing technique.

Again and again new techniques developed for more speed on the plain, the incline and the descent. Due to the current provision stating that competitions now have to be held separately in the classic style and freestyle (skating) and that techniques have been classified accordingly, new order has been brought to competitions. In this chapter, we will show you the most important cross-country skiing techniques, their distinctive features, what you have to pay attention to and which mistakes to avoid.

Trainers and sports scientists, as well as successful cross-country skiers always try to figure out which cross-country skiing technique is the best and the fastest. There are always in-novations and changes in execution. We have illustrated and described the currently most prevalent forms.

You will quickly adopt in-novations from top skiers or learn them from your trainer. Stay current and write or draw your notes in the appropriate places in this book.

THE CLASSIC TECHNIQUES

The diagonal stride

The diagonal stride is the most important technique in classic cross-country skiing. This technique is the one used most often by recreational athletes for "hiking," as well as in cross-country ski sport for high speed. With this stride, you can manage most of the course on the plain, in slightly undulating terrain, and moderate inclines.

- *You bend your knees slightly and prepare to push off.*
- *At the same time, your center of gravity shifts forward slightly – almost like you are falling.*
- *Your weight is on the push-off leg and you are searching for the pressure point.*

- *You forcefully push off to the rear.*
- *To do so, the push-off leg extends explosively from the hip, knee and ankle.*

This technique will still work for you in heavy, wet snow and when suffering strong fatigue. Elements of the diagonal stride are also an important part of other forms of techniques.

On steeper inclines, the diagonal stride turns into *bounding*. To get the best push-off and a good glide, the skis have to be waxed very well.

- *The push-off phase has ended when the torso and the push-off leg form a line.*

- *You glide on the other leg.*

- *When the push-off leg swings forward again, the pole is planted and "pulls" the body forward.*

The phases of the diagonal stride

In the diagonal stride, the skier constantly alternates between push-off and glide phases.

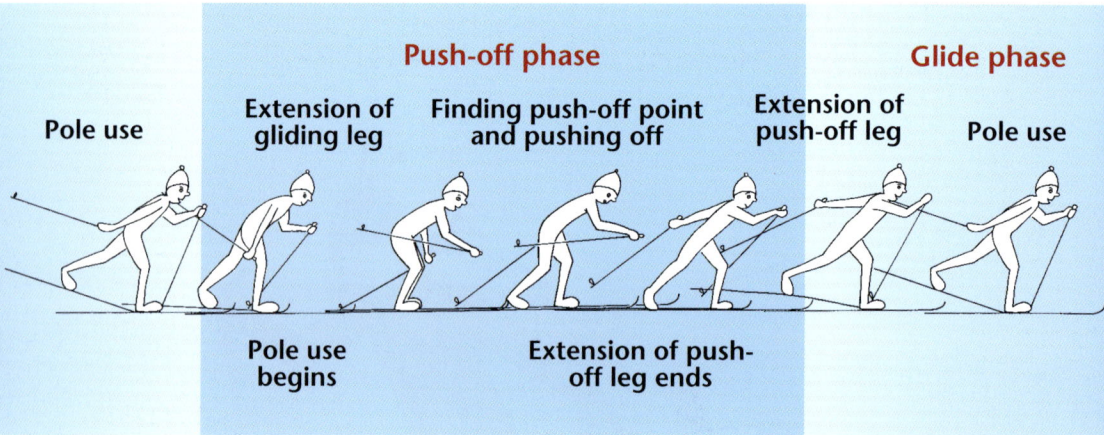

| Pole use | Extension of gliding leg | Finding push-off point and pushing off | Extension of push-off leg | Pole use |

Push-off phase — **Glide phase**

Pole use begins — Extension of push-off leg ends

What we mean by diagonal

In geometry, a straight line that connects two non-contiguous corners of a square is called a diagonal. Now imagine your arms and legs as corners of a square.

The diagonal movement is a totally natural motion sequence that we do almost automatically. We walk and run that way and even toddlers, when they crawl, use the

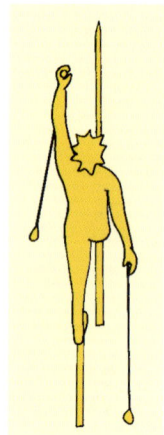

right leg with the left arm — **left arm with the right leg.**

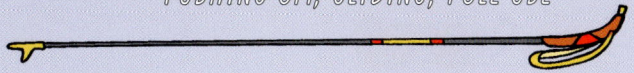

When doing the diagonal stride, you must avoid the following mistakes:

• *The arm push-off already ends at thigh level*

• *The hands pass the legs above the knees*

Which mistakes are the skiers making in the diagonal stride?
(see page 145 for answers)

Double poling

Double poling is a particularly important and very frequently used skiing technique. It is used especially on flat, slightly descending and undulating terrain. It is also a safe technique in difficult passages (narrow places, ice, etc.), is used to increase speed and allows for relaxation of the leg muscles during certain phases of a competition.

- *The torso is erect.*

- *The arms are parallel and swing forward easily.*

- *Almost on your toes, you feel a slight pressure on the balls of your feet.*

- *The knees are slightly bent and the poles are planted near the front part of the skies.*

- *The torso is bent.*

- *You try to put as much weight as possible on the poles.*

The double poling technique is strictly gliding. In doing so, the poles are planted simultaneously. Using strength and your whole upper body, you push yourself forward. The skis glide evenly.

This technique requires a lot of strength, but is also fast.

- *The arm pull is supported by the upper body action.*

- *The rear should not be pushed too far out back.*

- *The hands pass the legs slightly below the knees.*
- *After finishing the arm push-off, the arms loosely swing to the rear.*

The phases of double poling

When double poling, the skier constantly alternates between propulsion and glide phases.

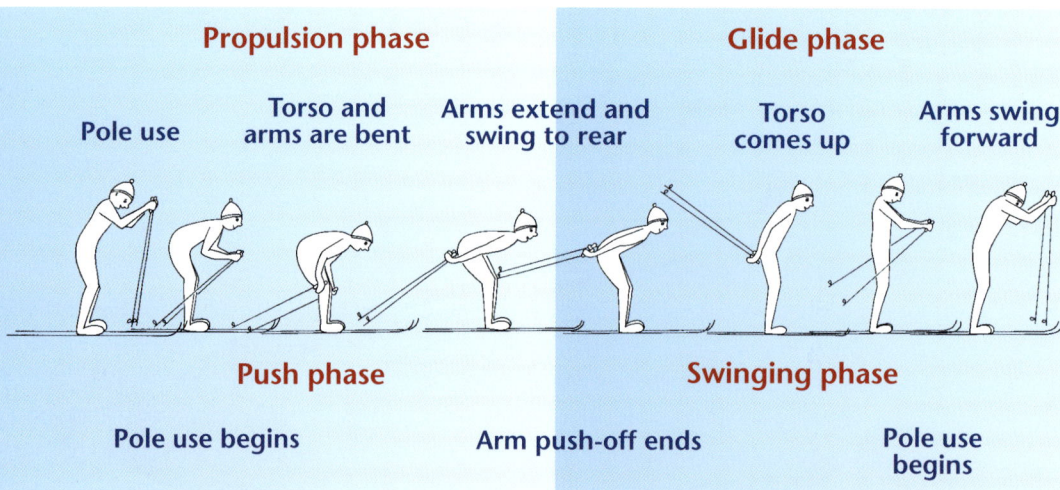

Propulsion phase			Glide phase	
Pole use	Torso and arms are bent	Arms extend and swing to rear	Torso comes up	Arms swing forward

Push phase		Swinging phase	
Pole use begins	Arm push-off ends		Pole use begins

This is how you can advantageously impact your double poling

Every skier continually tries to perfect his technique to be as fast as possible in a race. For that he tries to see, for instance, at which height the pole use is most effective, how long the glide phase should be or how low the torso must bend, etc. Varying the **foot position** is another option.

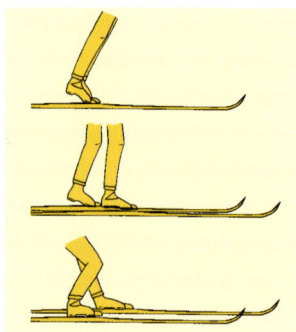

You can **straighten the ankle**, get up on the balls of your feet, and thereby shift your center of gravity even farther forward.

A slight **stride position** during the arm-swinging phase also shifts the center of gravity farther forward.

A **jet movement** is the pushing forward of one lower leg toward the end of the arm push-off. This is intended to give the ski more speed and extend the arm push-off.

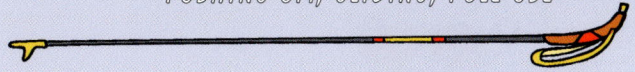

When double poling, you must avoid the following mistakes:

• During the push-off, the arms are not fully extended to the rear.

• The hands pass the legs above the knees.

Which mistakes are these skiers making while double poling?
(see page 145 for answers)

Double poling with kick

Double poling with kick is used in slightly rising terrain or on a level track when the gliding conditions are no longer good enough for single poling. This technique is also advantageous in undulating terrain. While skiing, the push-off for the kick occurs at the lowest spot of the depression. By utilizing the tension of the ski, the thrust effect is increased considerably.

- *You glide on both skis.*

- *The knees are slightly bent.*
- *You swing your arms forward.*

- *You slide the push-off leg a little ahead of the other leg.*
- *The push-off leg is vigorously extended back.*

- *The weight on the push-off leg increases.*
- *The gliding leg is straightened after the leg push-off is finished.*

With this technique, you are better able to accelerate and increase your speed than by single poling.

Double poling with kick is a combination of the diagonal stride and double poling. The skier must have a good command of the technique and excellent coordination. The legwork largely matches that of the diagonal stride. Alternating legs, the skier pushes off evenly. The pole action is very vigorous.

- *Body and arms extend forward.*

- *This shifts the center of gravity forward.*

- *The pole insertion angle is less then 90.°*

- *The pole action is vigorous and carries much momentum.*

- *The torso bends down very low.*

- *The arms swing out to the rear.*

The phases of double poling with kick

When double poling with kick, the skier constantly alternates between propulsion and glide phases.

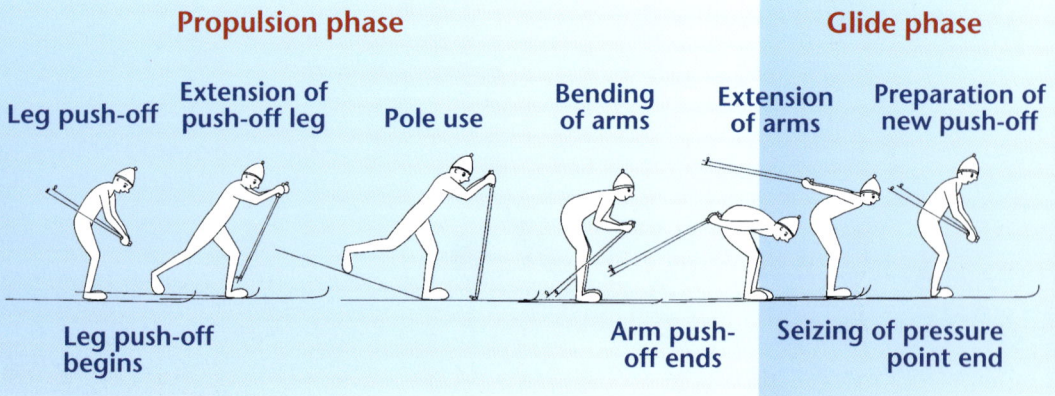

Propulsion phase				Glide phase	
Leg push-off · **Extension of push-off leg** · **Pole use**	**Bending of arms**		**Extension of arms**	**Preparation of new push-off**	

Leg push-off begins

Arm push-off ends

Seizing of pressure point end

Body position

During pole use, the body is nearly erect. After the skier vigorously pushes off with the poles, the arms are extended back. In doing so, the upper body is bent approximately 90°.

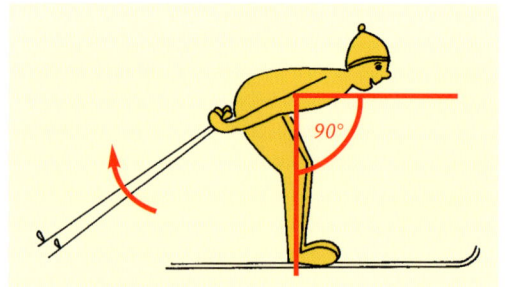

90°

This is what you need to pay attention to:

❄ The leg push-off is vigorous and explosive.
❄ The arms energetically swing forward into starting position at shoulder level.
❄ The free leg energetically swings forward.
❄ During the glide phase, the hip position is high.

When double poling with kick, the following mistakes must be avoided:

- You end the forward swing of the legs too soon and therefore have trouble coordinating the movements.

- Your arm push-off is too weak; you prematurely stop the arm action or after pushing off, the arms knock together in the back.

Which mistakes are these skiers making while double poling with kick?
(see page 145 for answers)

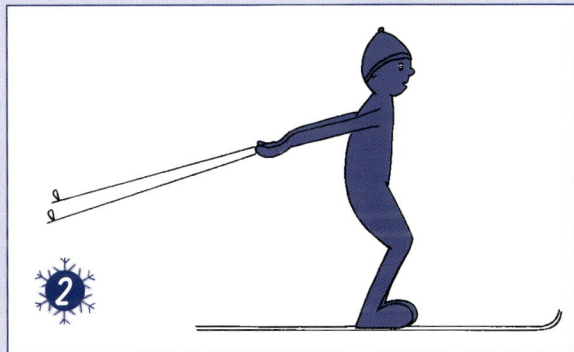

ON A HILL

The herringbone

You use the herringbone climb when you are no longer able to manage the incline of a hill with the diagonal stride and bounding.

- *You push off with your right leg and move the other leg forward sideways.*

- *The left pole pushes off when the right leg pushes off.*

- *During the push-off and forward movement the right arm swings forward.*

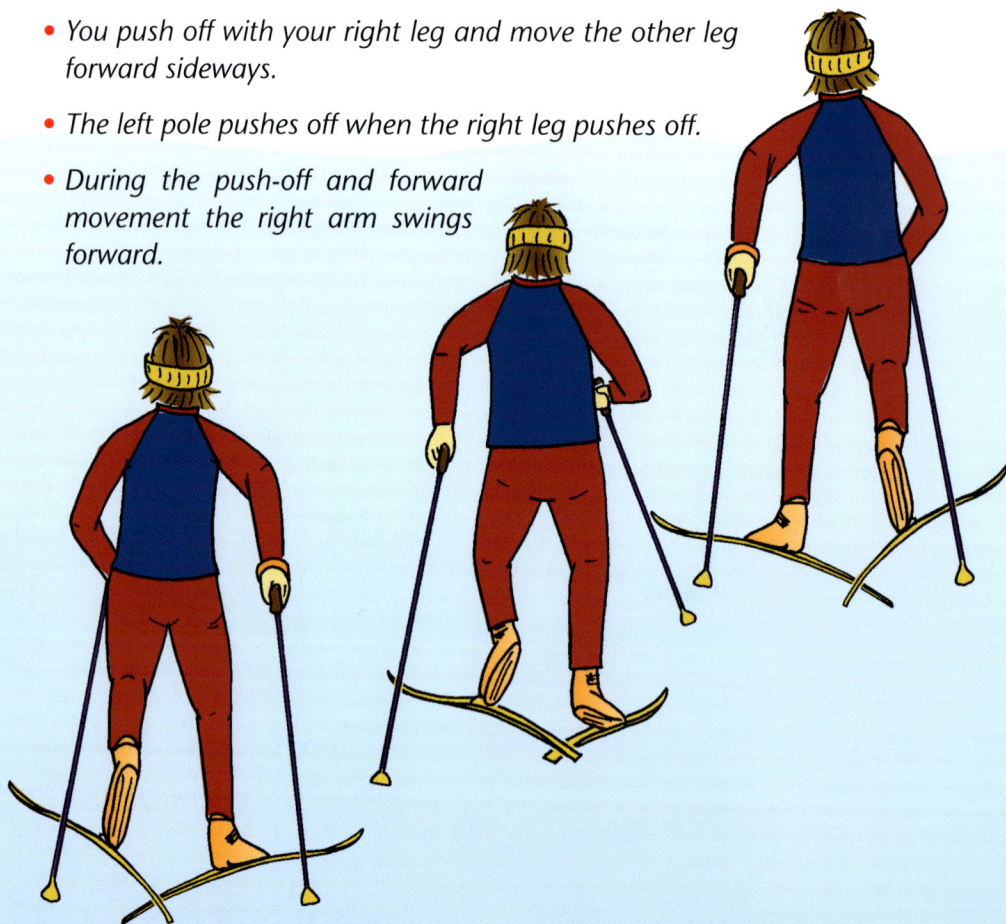

The alternate movement of arms and legs is the same as that of the diagonal stride, only the skis are turned out sideways in a straddle position and set on the inside edges. The push-off is done primarily with the inside edge.

Variation

If the hill is too steep and it is not possible to get a good push-off, you should switch over to the bounding herringbone climb. But that only makes sense if you are not too exhausted from the race yet and have a sufficient strength reserve.

The half-herringbone

If the groove is still there on the incline, you can also manage it in a half-herringbone. But that can only be done if you can get enough traction to push off. This technique is also used when the track "dips" to one side. Here the downhill ski is turned out.

When you have barely enough strength left in an exhausting race, your legs get "heavy" and you start to slip, the half-herringbone is the ideal solution on a hill.

- *Propulsion is achieved via the leg push-off with the right leg and the simultaneous left pole push-off.*

- *Then the left ski moves forward and is turned out sideways and the right arm swings forward.*

- *Propulsion is achieved via the push-off from the left ski and the right pole push-off.*

- *The eyes always look straight ahead.*

In a classic style competition, only the bounding herringbone and half-herringbone are permitted. The international rules of competition regarding classic technique specify that there cannot be a gliding phase in the execution of the herringbone.

CHANGING DIRECTION

Step turning

This is a technique for changing direction in the classic technique. It is used on the plain and in ascending turns. In doing so, the diagonal stride motion is maintained.

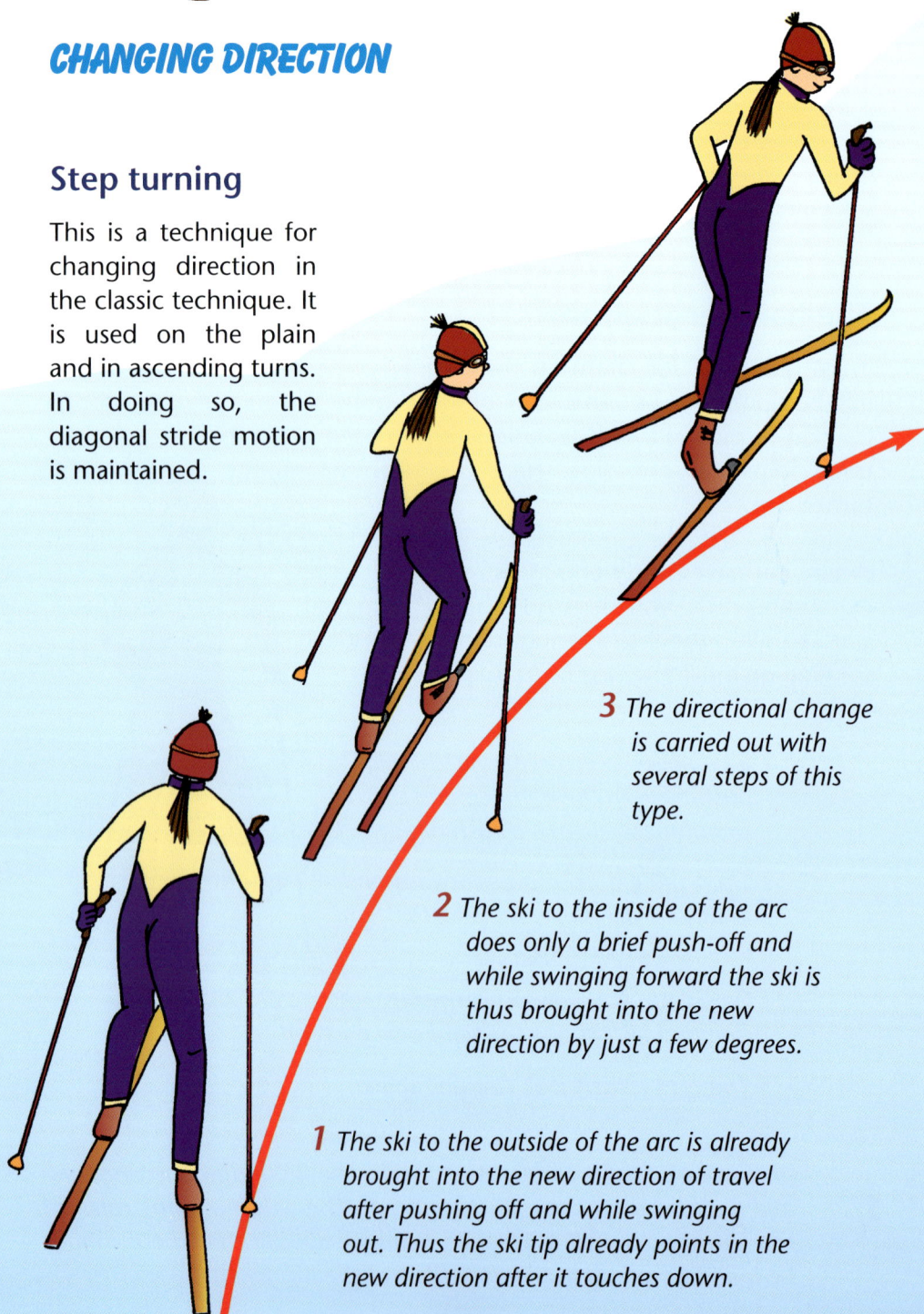

3 The directional change is carried out with several steps of this type.

2 The ski to the inside of the arc does only a brief push-off and while swinging forward the ski is thus brought into the new direction by just a few degrees.

1 The ski to the outside of the arc is already brought into the new direction of travel after pushing off and while swinging out. Thus the ski tip already points in the new direction after it touches down.

106

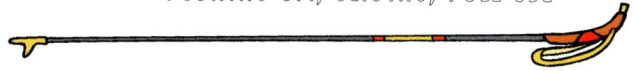

Special characteristics

While step turning, you can maintain the rhythm of movement of the diagonal stride. The glide phases and stride lengths become shorter, but you take quicker steps.

The track image

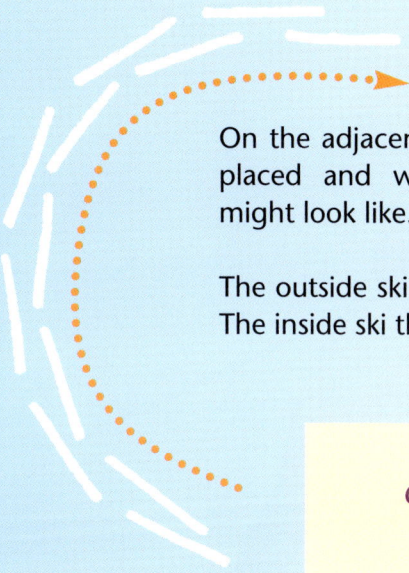

On the adjacent image you can see how the skis are placed and what the corresponding track image might look like.

The outside ski is brought into the new direction first. The inside ski then follows.

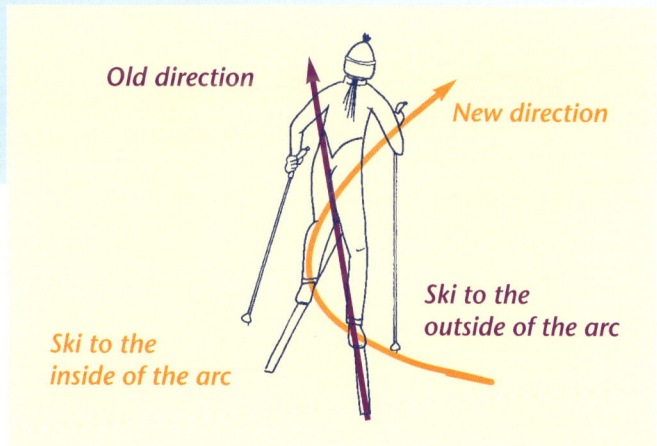

Old direction

New direction

Ski to the outside of the arc

Ski to the inside of the arc

Depending on the turn radius, the body assumes a slightly curved position while step turning.

THE FREE TECHNIQUES

This cross-country skiing technique, also referred to as *skate stride* or *skating*, facilitates a higher skiing speed than the classic style. The skier uses a special skating ski (glide ski) that does not require any kick wax at all. For execution of the skating technique, the course (track) must be well prepared. That means the snow is smooth and firmly packed.

To achieve propulsion the skier pushes off vigorously with the ski that is turned out at an angle to the skiing direction. Most of the time this is supported by vigorous double poling.

- *The poles are tucked under the arms.*

- *The upper body is bent.*

- *You look straight ahead.*

- *The left leg pushes off vigorously and explosively with the inside ski edge.*

- *After pushing off, the push-off leg is almost straight.*

Skate stride without poling

This motion sequence is well known from ice skating or inline skating. It can also be used with alpine skis on a plain.

The cross-country skier uses this technique when gliding conditions are very good and while moving at a high speed on downhill stretches or on a plain. Then the step sequence becomes too fast for the poles to be useful and poling is therefore not necessary. In fact, it often is an impediment. The skier carries the poles high and does the skate stride without poling.

- *You straighten up a little to switch legs.*
- *The hip is positioned over the gliding leg.*

- *Now the right leg pushes off vigorously.*
- *You glide on the left leg.*
- *The center of gravity is now over the left leg.*

The track image

The track image shows the ski tracks at an angle with the fronts pointing to the outside and no pole impressions.

The variations

When doing the skate stride without poling you have various options for holding your arms and poles. It depends on the conditions.

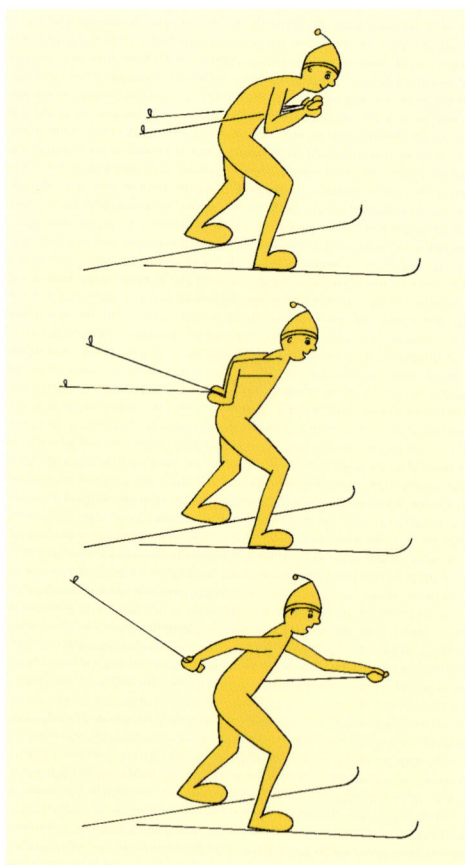

Variation "downhill"
The poles are tucked under the arms and the body remains relatively still.

Variation "speed skating"
Here, the arms are held behind the back, like in speed skating. The poles are held back and up.

Variation "finish"
Here the arms swing in a diagonal rhythm to the legs, thus lending additional support to the alternate shifting of the load

The skate stride without poling is also very important in the biathlon. Shortly before reaching the shooting range, the skiers have to forgo the use of their poles to relieve the strain on their arms.

Gliding

The balance constantly shifts. The center of gravity is always over the respective gliding leg.

The gliding leg is extended.

Hip position is high.

Due to the constant shifting of the center of gravity, the gliding action often occurs only on the inside edge of the ski.

The skis have to briefly overlap.

Gliding direction

Direction of travel

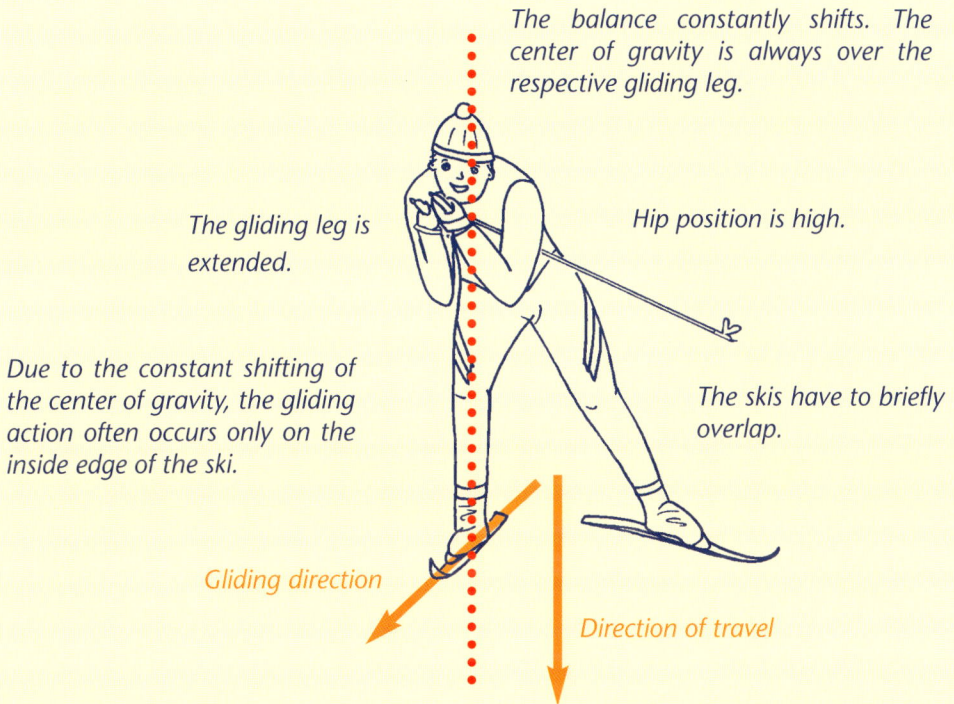

At very high speeds, like during the finish, the glide phases and the glide angle are shortened. The gliding leg is also no longer extended all the way.

Skate stride and double poling with every leg push-off, 1:1

If you want to go faster, or the speed is too low for the skate stride without poling, put your poles to use. Vigorous double poling with every leg-push-off will let you pick up speed.

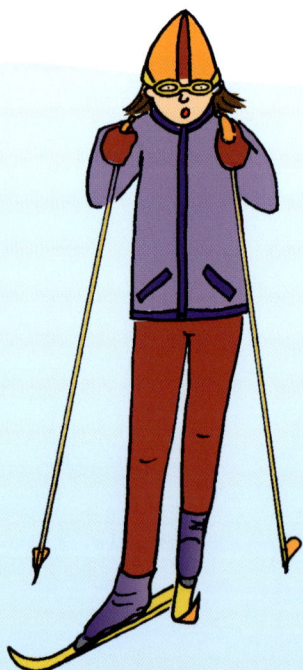

- *The left ski is brought forward.*

- *Both arms come forward, parallel.*

- *To push off with your poles, plant them in front of the binding.*

- *Before pushing off, the right ski is set on edge.*

- *You push off vigorously with the right leg.*

- *You glide on the left leg. The gliding leg is almost completely extended.*

- *After pushing off with the arms, the poles swing back past the body until they reach the reversal point.*

This technique is used when the track and snow conditions are good and the terrain is flat or slightly sloping. Competitive athletes also use this technique on slight inclines.

The center of gravity constantly shifts from the push-off leg to the gliding leg.

- *The push-off leg is brought back even to the gliding leg.*

- *You swing the arms forward into starting position.*

- *At the same time, straighten up, assuming a high hip position.*

- *Now the left ski is put on edge for the push-off.*

- *You push off vigorously with the left ski and glide on the right ski.*

- *Another arm push-off is executed.*

Skate stride with energetic arm swing, 2:1 (symmetrical)

This technique, in which the poles are only used with every second leg push-off, is the definitive skating technique for skiing with speed on flat terrain. Symmetrical means that the poles are planted on a level. It is an

- *In the starting position, your body is erect and the hips are high.*

- *The center of gravity is shifted slightly forward. The weight is on the left leg – the gliding leg.*

- *The poles are planted simultaneously next to the binding.*

- *After the push-off, the center of gravity shifts to the other leg.*

- *During the glide phase, the poles swing out to the back.*

aesthetic style of skiing that requires very good balance and perfect coordination between arm and leg work.

This technique has a number of different names and also a variety of execution styles. The skier can use the poles always when pushing off with the left leg or always when pushing off with the right leg.

2:1 (asymmetrical)

On relatively steep inclines, tracks with dips, poor gliding conditions or when losing strength, skiers often switch over to the asymmetrical variation. It can be distinguished by the climbing forward of one leg and the unilaterally heightened pole work. You can recognize this on the track image. The planting of the poles occurs simultaneously, level with the binding respectively – but slightly offset. The pole push-off and leg push-off also occur at the same time.

- *You straighten up again during the glide phase.*
- *The push-off with the other leg occurs without using the poles.*
- *The poles return to the front into starting position.*

1:1 Each leg push-off is followed by a double pole push-off.

2:1 – Symmetrical   *The arm work, with the arms swinging forward energetically, and the leg work occur simultaneously.*

2:1 – Asymmetrical   *The arm push-off and the leg push-off occur simultaneously on a definite driving side.*

Track images

The track image of the *skate stride with double pole push-off* (1:1) can be distinguished by the ski tracks that are angled outward and one pole impression for every leg push-off.

The track image of the *skate stride with energetic arm swing (2:1) symmetrical* can be distinguished by the ski tracks that are angled outward and the parallel pole impressions with every second leg push-off.

With (2:1) *asymmetrical,* you can see the offset pole impressions and the driving side.

Alternating sides

For a consistent strain on muscles, but also when the course requires it, you must always alternate the side of the push-off leg when using the skate stride techniques. On tracks that dip, it is always the downhill ski and in turns it is always the outside ski that serves as the push-off ski.

The half-skate stride

The cross-country skier always uses his technique to adapt to the terrain and course conditions. If the course requires it, also use the *half-skate stride* to avoid disrupting the skiing rhythm. In doing so, the push-off ski is always placed back in the groove after the leg push-off. After the double pole push-off, the other ski sheers out for the leg push-off.

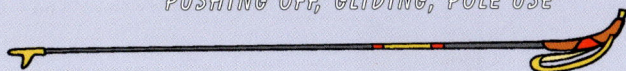

When doing the skate stride, the following mistakes must be avoided:

- The center of gravity is not totally shifted to the gliding leg.
- The glide phase is cut short and the speed is thus reduced.

Which mistakes are the skiers making in the skate stride?
(see page 145 for answers)

Skate-turning

At high speeds on a plain or on a downhill stretch, there are often turns. You want to ski through them without losing speed. On the contrary, you want to gain speed if possible. That is why it is important to master the skate-turning technique. This technique belongs to the group of skate-stride techniques and can therefore only be used at freestyle events.

- *The center of gravity is over the outside ski.*

- *The ski to the outside of the arc is put on its inside edge.*

- *You are already looking in the new direction.*

- *The ski to the inside of the arc sheers out into the new direction*

- *The outside edging ski pushes off vigorously into the new direction.*

- *The weight is now shifted from the outside ski to the inside ski – the gliding ski.*

- *Subsequently the outside ski returns to the inside ski.*

The track image

The adjacent illustration shows how the skis are placed and what the corresponding track image might look like.

While the ski to the inside of the arc is placed in the new direction first, the ski to the outside of the arc remains in the old direction for the time being. Then it follows behind.

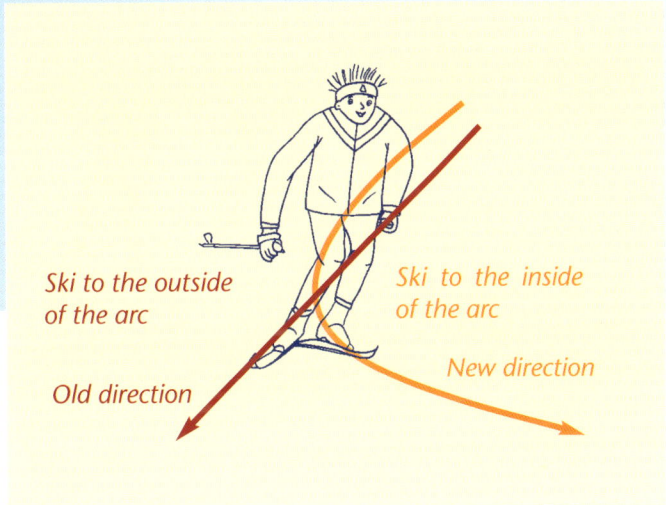

Ski to the outside of the arc

Ski to the inside of the arc

New direction

Old direction

Variations

❄ At high speeds, or in narrow turns, it is better to skate-turn *without using poles*. You won't have enough time for a double pole push-off.

❄ At lower speeds, or on flat terrain, you can support the skate-turning with a *double pole push-off* during the glide phase and thus increase your speed.

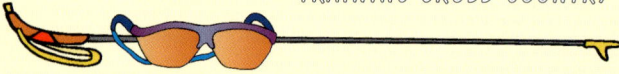

THIS IS HOW YOU CAN PRACTICE

What makes the skate stride unique is that you always push off with one leg and glide with the other leg. This alternation between pushing off and gliding, of the right leg and the left leg, also shifts your center of gravity. You glide on one leg and the other leg is moved up for the next push-off and set on edge.

To do this, you need a good sense of balance and coordination. You can practice and improve that in winter and in summer, with skis or without skis.

Skiing without poles

To gain a good perception of your body, you should also practice unusual movements during training. For instance, while keeping your skis parallel, or during the skate stride, you could perform the following movements:

- *Hold your arms out in front, extend your arms up, wave, swim*
- *Walk markedly straight or bent over, like a robot or a dancer*
- *Perform the push-off and glide phase with a lot of exaggeration.*
- *How about a little dance performance – like figure skating?*

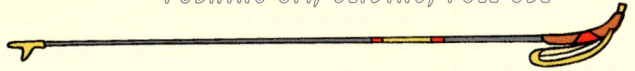

Glide phases

Feel how long the glide phase should be in order to achieve the highest speed.

- *Glide on one leg until you almost come to a stop.*
- *Make the glide phase very short.*
- *Glide on the downhill ski on a course that dips, and then glide on the uphill ski.*
- *Glide on one leg past an obstacle.*

Changing grooves and direction

Perform these exercises on a plain, in sloping terrain and going downhill.

- *Change grooves with one or two steps sideways and back (hiking in the grooves).*
- *Change grooves by jumping in the next groove.*
- *Change grooves on command: "Now!" "Jump!" "Left!" "Right!" "Double right!" etc. with a training buddy.*
- *Respond to commands while going downhill: "Right-right-left-right-right-right-left-left-left-left ...!"*

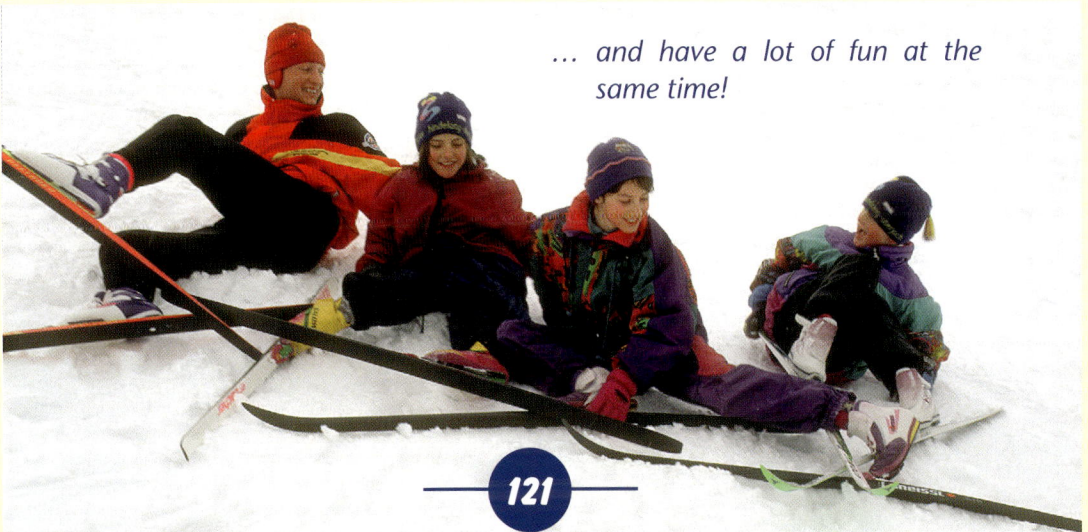

... and have a lot of fun at the same time!

THE IMPORTANT ROLLER SKI TRAINING

"World champions are made during the summer!" is a well-known saying in skiing circles.

Cross-country skiing is strictly a winter sport. That is when all of the season highlights take place and everyone can show off what they've got on the cross-country course. But that does not in any way imply that there is a training break during the snow-less season. The foundations for endurance and strength are laid during summer training. That has already been emphasized in chapter 9, "Training Plan".

But roller ski training also allows you to practice that specific technique in a competition-like way. With roller ski training for classic technique as well as for skate technique and with the aid of poles with special tips, you can practice and improve arm push-offs, leg push-offs, rhythm, etc., on asphalt courses.

Your trainer will know a variety of exercises and can point out the particularities of skiing with roller skis.

11 SNOW, SKIS, WAX

The best cross-country ski teams in the world have, aside from their trainers, an entire service team behind them. The best material for any snow and track conditions is chosen and prepped for the athletes. Constant testing is being done to determine which ski shape, which type of binding and which shoes are ideal. Experts research new materials, the best coatings and special waxes.

Scientists calculate the optimal ski length, pole length and material hardness based on the athlete's size, his movements and muscular exertion. The snow is analyzed and the appropriate ski and optimal wax sequence are found.

Working with ski materials, waxing techniques and snow conditions is very important for every skier. Every cross-country skier is responsible for the completeness and condition of his clothing, and his ski equipment, as well as choosing and prepping his skis. You often train by yourself and during the preparation phase of a competition the trainer has to look after all the athletes.

In this chapter we can only briefly discuss clothing, ski material and waxing. But it should peak your interest enough to find out more about it.

A LITTLE SNOW SCIENCE

To be able to choose the right skis, as well as to pick the right thing out of the wax box, you have to know something about how snow forms, its composition and deformation. When temperatures are below freezing, water vapor crystallizes to snow in the air. In doing so, a snow

crystal forms around a dust speck. All snow crystals are hexagonal when they form, but their deformation begins while still in the air. Due to the varying factors in the atmosphere, they transform into tiny plates, balls ... even needles. This deformation continues on the ground, depending on wind, humidity, temperatures and how long it has been on the ground. Its granulation, moisture content and porosity (density) are determining factors in its classification as a type of dry snow or wet snow.

Dry snow

Powder snow:
Dry, needle-like crystals, very porous snow cover.

Flour snow:
Wind-pressed snow, fine grained, broken crystals, partially compressed snow cover.

Flinty snow:
Semolina or salt kernel-size, rounded crystals of powder snow that has been on the ground for some time, during fluctuating temperatures and humidity.

Hoar frost snow:
Hoar frost, plate-like crystals, forms on the snow-cover, on trees and shrubs, due to high humidity and cold temperatures.

Crusty snow:
Up to pea-sized ice crystals, frozen together to form snow cover, forms by melting and refreezing multiple times.

Wet snow

Sticky snow:
Moist, fine grained, forms from powder snow when warm.

Wet gritty snow:
Round crystals, very moist due to rain and temperature fluctuations.

Wet hoar frost snow:
Very moist granules, plates and rod-shaped crystals, forms during prolonged rain, high humidity and temperatures around 32° F.

Firn:
Coarse, round, pea-sized ice crystals, forms from crusty snow when temperature rises.

Slush:
Highly moist firn that has softened all the way to the ground due to sun or rain, quite dirty, the last snow before snow-melt.

THE RIGHT CROSS-COUNTRY SKI

Due to the different techniques, competitive skiers need a wax ski for classic technique and a gliding ski (skate ski) for freestyle, the skating technique. Add to that the various types of snow that require either a dry snow ski or a wet snow ski. For a cross-country skier who wants to start in both competitions it means:

Classic technique:	Wax ski	–	dry snow ski
	Wax ski	–	wet snow ski
Freestyle technique:	Fine structure	–	dry snow
	Coarse structure	–	wet snow

The differences between wax skis and skate skis

The key criterion here is the often-mentioned leg push-off. It is essential so you can perform the cross-country skiing technique in a way that allows you to gain speed and acceleration.

With the **wax ski,** the push-off occurs in the area below the binding. The ski has so much tension that the bottom of the ski only makes contact with the track when there is weight on the ski. During this brief contact, the snow crystals are pressed into the special wax coating (kick wax), making it possible to push off against the direction of travel and thus facilitate propulsion. On a wax ski, the glide zones are located in the front and back areas. Good gliding is possible once the wax-coated center of the ski no longer has weight on it.

Glide zone　　　*Push-off zone*　　　*Glide zone*

The skate ski is faster because the entire length of the ski is used for pushing off. Propulsion occurs through vigorous, dynamic pushing off from the track with the inside edge of the turned out ski. The push-off impulse is longer and the skiing speed is therefore higher. The skate ski is more stable and built with less tension. A push-off zone in the binding area and kick wax are not necessary. Gliding takes place with the entire length of the ski. The skate ski is shorter than the wax ski.

Dry ski and wet ski

Snow has different degrees of hardness, different forms and thus also different gliding properties. There is a simple rule for that: Soft snow – soft coatings (graphite), hard snow – hard coatings (transparent coatings)! Since it is not technically possible to change the coatings according to the snow conditions, it is good to have two sets of ski material. For skate skis, new glide waxes (paraffin) and new treatment methods like grinds or groove patterns on the bottom of the ski nowadays also make possible a good response in dry and wet snow conditions.

The correct lengths

Wax ski

Length:	Approx. 20-30 cm (8-12 inches) + body height
Surface tension:	Medium, soft or hard – depending on body weight

Skate ski

Length:	Approx. 10-15 cm (4-6 inches) + body height
Surface tension:	Soft or hard – depending on body weight

Poles

Classic:	Body height x 0.8
Skating:	Body height x 0.9

Take care of your cross-country skis and keep them in good condition! Avoid damage to the skis' base and edges. The skis must be waxed and prepped every 25 to 50 miles.

LITTLE WAX SCIENCE

Just like the different types of snow and the ongoing advancements in ski materials, you should also learn something early on about "the art of waxing." The sooner you start, the more experience you will get and the more confident you will be later when choosing a certain wax. Use your training diary and document the current snow condition, the wax you chose for it and the experiences at training and competition, for the duration of your active cross-country skiing career. Armed with this knowledge, you will always have an advantage!

What belongs in the "wax box":

- Snow thermometer, iron, wax iron.
- Wax remover, spatula, stripping blades, brushes, sandpaper.
- Wax corks, brush, cleaning cloths, spatula.
- Wax assortment with glide waxes (paraffin), hard waxes and klister.

Prior to the actual waxing of the skis on competition day, the skis must be prepped (the day before):

1. **Cleaning** the base.
2. **Waxing** (glide zone with glide wax), iron in, scrape out the center groove.
3. **Stripping** the ironed-on wax with a plastic blade in skiing direction.
4. **Brushing off** with a suitable brush, brush off the coating down to the recognizable structure (grooves)
5. **Cleaning and roughening** the grip zone on a classic ski with fine gauge sandpaper. In doing so, watch the push-off zone and polish.

Get some advice from your parents, your trainer or another expert!

Colors help

The manufacturers of **ski waxes** largely adhere to the generally accepted color rules:

from -10° C from 14°F	-5 to -10° C 21°F to 14°F	-2 to -5° C 28°F to 21°F	around 0° C/32°F	around 0° C/32°F

There has always been a similar classification for klister waxes, which is no longer very reliable.

Skare around -8°C/ 18°F	around -5°C/21°F	around -3°C/ 26°F	Mixed snow	above 0°C/32°F	far above 0°C/32°F

A few tips

Hard waxes for dry snow.
Soft waxes for wet snow.
Glide waxes and glide zones for skate skis.

The finer the snow crystal, the harder the wax.
The coarser the crystal, the softer the wax.

The colder and dryer the snow, the harder the wax.
The warmer and wetter the snow, the softer the wax.

The firmer the groove, the smoother the wax.
The looser the groove, the more traction the wax should have. (There are exceptions.)

The thicker the wax layer, the more traction the ski has, the slower the ski is.
The thinner the wax layer, the smoother and faster the ski.

The softer the track, the softer the ski tension.
The harder the track, the harder the ski tension.

Watch the weather and check the snow in the groove. Famous cross-country skiers publish their wax experiences in so called "wax primers." Pick one up! Ask your trainer about detailed wax tables!

CLOTHING

The skier is outside in the cold; he moves and sweats. That is very hard on his clothing.

The athlete wants
- ❄ to be warm.
- ❄ to be able to move comfortably.
- ❄ to have less wind resistance with tight-fitting clothes.
- ❄ the moisture to be wicked away from his body.

The "magic word" is **functional clothing**! This type of clothing consists of a special material that absorbs and wicks the body's moisture. The outer layer must lend protection from wind and snow. Depending on the outside temperature, warming layers are worn in between.

The **hat** should be made from breathable material. Put it on so your body heat does not escape through your head like a chimney. Make sure that your ears are well protected against wind and cold.

Protect your face with a **skin cream that contains oil**. Make sure it isn't a moisturizer, because the water it contains can freeze. Use sunscreen if necessary.

The right **gloves** keep your hands warm, are non-slip for a good grip, and protect you from injuries.

The **darkened glasses** must be non-breakable and non-slip and can't fog up. They protect the eyes from too much light in the snow and from the sun's UV-rays. But you are also protected from injury by, for instance, the pole of a skier in front of you. If you need glasses for vision acuity, get advice from your optometrist.

A **scarf or a neck gator** over your mouth will protect you from the cold air while breathing. Do not use a cotton scarf because the moisture will make it freeze, and it will get hard and stiff.

Pack fresh clothes in your gym bag! You should change out of wet clothes as soon as possible. Quickly getting undressed and dressed outside is better than training in wet clothes.

There is no such thing as bad weather – only unsuitable clothing!

"WHAT'S GOING ON WITH YOU, PAUL?
YOU ALWAYS SEEM SO SLEEPY DURING PRACTICE!"
"DON'T WORRY, COACH!
THAT'S JUST MY GREAT LATENT TALENT!"

THE VISITOR ASKS MAX,
"WHEN DO YOU EAT LUNCH AROUND HERE?"
"ALWAYS AT NOON, EXCEPT WHEN WE HAVE VISITORS –
THEN WE WAIT UNTIL THEY LEAVE!"

EVERYONE IS SKIING THE DOWNHILL STRETCH
WITH A SHARP TURN EXCEPT FOR TINA.
THE OTHERS CALL OUT TO HER: "GUESS YOU'RE SCARED!"
"NO, I'M NOT! BUT SOMETIMES
YOU JUST HAVE TO CONTROL YOURSELF!"

12 KEEPING THINGS STRAIGHT

Almost everything in people's lives is regulated. It would be pretty chaotic if everyone did whatever they want anytime, anywhere. Living together as a family usually involves following certain rules, and so does going to school. There are traffic rules for motor vehicles, and every game is played by rules.

The sport of skiing takes place in a special environment that has to be protected and taken care of. There are important rules every skier needs to know and adhere to so everyone has fun, no one is hurt and nature is protected.

In addition, there are regulations that specify the ski material and the skiing technique, and of course prohibit the use of performance-enhancing drugs. A competition is fun when it is fair and all of the participants play by the rules.

Learn about the rules regarding tracks, courses and lifts. Someone who loves nature also cares about its preservation.

THE FIS RULES OF CONDUCT

1 Respect for others
Every cross-country skier must behave in such a way that he does not endanger or prejudice others.

2 Signs, direction of travel and skiing technique
Signs and signals (informational signs) must be respected. On tracks and runs, skiers must travel in the specified direction and skiing technique.

3 Choosing a groove and a track
On double and multiple grooves, skiers must use the groove on the right. Cross-country skiers in groups must ski astride in the groove on the right. Freestyle skiers must use the right side of the track.

4 Passing
Passing is allowed on the left and on the right. The front skier does not have to give way. However, he should give way if he can do so safely.

5 Two-way traffic
When encountering other skiers, everyone must give way to the right. The skier going downhill has the right of way.

6 Pole etiquette

When passing, being passed, and when encountering other skiers, the poles should be carried close to the body.

7 Adapting of speed to prevailing conditions

Every cross-country skier must adapt his speed and manner of skiing to his personal ability, the prevailing conditions of terrain, density of traffic and visibility. He must maintain a safe distance to the skier ahead of him. If necessary, he must fall down to avoid a collision.

8 Keeping grooves and tracks clear

Anyone who stops, must get out of the groove or off the track. A cross-country skier who has fallen down must clear the groove/track as quickly as possible.

9 Assistance

At accident, every skier is duty bound to assist.

10 Identification

Every skier, whether witness or involved party, must exchange names and addresses following an accident.

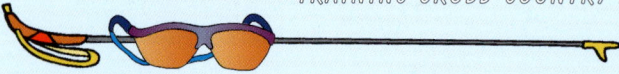

Just like in road traffic, there are danger signs and prohibition signs on the track, the run and at lift installations. The statement can be easily recognized by the symbol.

What do these two signs mean? Write it down!

1

2

_____   _____

Learn about other signs that alert you to dangers and noteworthy situations!

What do you think about Snowman's attitude?
(see page 145 for answers)

HEY, YOU CAN'T JUST THROW THAT SODA CAN IN THE SNOW! THROW IT IN THE WASTE BASKET OR TAKE IT HOME!

IT'S NOT A PROBLEM! SOON IT WILL SNOW AGAIN AND YOU WON'T EVEN SEE IT!

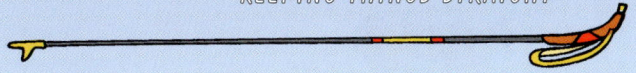

SKIERS ARE NATURE LOVERS

Not many athletes are fortunate enough to be so close to nature. As a skier, you experience the beauty of the mountains, the snow and the fresh, healthy winter air.

But there are also many nature lovers who view the increasingly popular ski sport as a threat. They believe that young plants are snapped off by the traffic on the tracks and runs, that all of the activity disturbs the animals and that ski tourists leave a lot of trash behind. But it doesn't have to be that way. If every athlete behaves respectfully and considerately, loves nature and cares about its preservation, a positive relationship is possible.

The FIS Environmental Rules

The FIS has established environmental rules for winter sport athletes. Derived from these, the most important ones are listed here:

• Learn about your ski area.

• Support the areas in their care for the environment.

• Choose environmentally friendly modes of transportation, such as bus or train, for your trip to the resort.

• Carpool if you have to travel there by car.

• Ski and snowboard only if there is a sufficient snow cover.

• Stay on the marked runs.

• Respect signs and stay off closed runs.

• Do not ski or board off the runs, particularly in wooded areas.

• Do not ski or board in protected areas.

• Conserve wildlife and plants.

• Take your trash with you.

HAVE YOU HAD A LAUGH TODAY?

"IS THE WEATHER
REPORT RELIABLE?"
"YES, BUT THE DATE
IS SOMETIMES WRONG!"

THE TEACHER EXPLAINS:
"FROZEN LIMBS SHOULD BE RUBBED WITH SNOW!"
ASKS TONY: "AND IN THE SUMMER?"

TOM BUYS A HOTDOG AT THE SKI HUT.
NEXT IN LINE IS A SNOWMAN THAT SAYS:
"FRENCH FRIES WITH MAYO, PLEASE!"
SAYS TOM: "WELL, I'VE NEVER SEEN THAT BEFORE!"
ANSWERS THE VENDOR: "NEITHER HAVE I. USUALLY HE WANTS
KETCHUP WITH HIS FRIES!"

"WHAT WOULD YOU DO IF YOU
COULD SKI AS WELL AS I?"
"TAKE LESSONS!"

TOM SAYS TO TINA:
"YOU ARE WEARING ONE BLUE SHOE
AND ONE YELLOW SHOE!"
ANSWERS TINA:
"I KNOW, ISN'T IT STRANGE?
AND I HAVE ANOTHER PAIR JUST LIKE THAT
AT HOME, TOO!"

TWO SKIERS COLLIDE ON THE TRACK AND GET TANGLED UP.
ONE SKIER SHOUTS: "HELP, HELP – I CAN'T FEEL ONE OF MY LEGS!"
ANSWERS THE OTHER ONE: "I CAN SEE WHY! THAT'S MY LEG YOU KEEP PINCHING!"

. . . . *13 FIT AND HEALTHY*

Anyone who thinks that hard, sweaty training several times a week is enough for athletic success will soon learn better. Next to the demanding training, periods of recuperation are very important, as are plenty of sleep, good nutrition, physical hygiene, organization, and much more.

You should be familiar with your internal clock and learn to pay attention to it. It tells you when you are particularly fit or when you urgently need rest and should relax. A good skier, for instance, also senses when he needs some high-energy nutrition to maintain his performance capacity and concentration.

In this chapter, we have compiled some interesting information on this topic. Take this as an incentive to learn more about your internal clock, as well as good nutrition.

Have fun!

OUR PERFORMANCE CAPACITY

In the course of a day, our performance capacity experiences highs and lows, as you can see on the curve below. This is similar for all people, and we have adjusted our lives accordingly. Most school instruction is done in the morning, then some people even take a nap during lunch, in the afternoon we accelerate again, and at night our body gets its well-earned sleep. Anyone who follows this rhythm lives a healthy and productive life. You can feel it if you don't get enough rest and sufficient sleep, and it would be a shame not to utilize those physical "highs."

Eat and drink yourself fit

Athletes who eat or drink too much of the wrong things before training or a race are not efficient. They feel stuffed and appear tired and listless. Many body functions slow down because the stomach is working overtime. But we must eat and especially drink to replenish the body's used up energy and to balance the loss of fluids caused by sweating. It is also necessary to do so periodically during long training sessions and at strenuous competitions.

Look at this overview to see what is suitable for your main meals, snacks, and the in-between energy boost, and what isn't. Choose your foods and drinks, as well as the time of consumption, carefully so you are sufficiently satiated during training or at a competition, but are not still digesting.

How long foods stay in the stomach until they are digested:

Approx. one hour: Water, tea, broth.

Approx. 2 – 3 hours: Cocoa, banana, apple, roll, rice, cooked fish, soft boiled egg, whole grain bread.

Approx. 4 – 5 hours: Sausage, meat, fried potatoes, French fries, beans or peas.

Approx. 6- 7 hours: Layer cake, mushrooms, fish in oil, fatty roast.

The food pyramid shows which foods you should eat in large quantities (very bottom) and which you should preferably eat very rarely (very top). Examples are given for each food group.

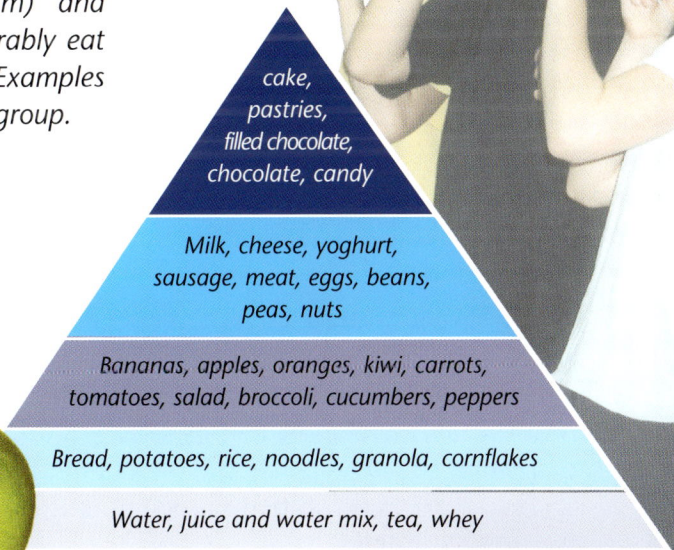

cake,
pastries,
filled chocolate,
chocolate, candy

Milk, cheese, yoghurt,
sausage, meat, eggs, beans,
peas, nuts

Bananas, apples, oranges, kiwi, carrots,
tomatoes, salad, broccoli, cucumbers, peppers

Bread, potatoes, rice, noodles, granola, cornflakes

Water, juice and water mix, tea, whey

If you sweat, you have to drink a lot

To balance the loss of fluids from sweating, you have to drink enough fluids during training and competition. Otherwise your performance capacity drops, your blood thickens and absorbs less oxygen, and you will get muscle cramps.

❄ **Suitable beverages before and during exertion**
Water, juice and water mix in proportions of 1:3, lightly sweetened beverages.

❄ **Suitable beverages after exertion**
Juice and water mix with a higher juice ratio, milk smoothies, beverages with higher sugar content.

Cross-country skiers need to drink, especially on long racecourses. For this, there are hardworking helpers or drinking stations. You should definitely not skip these – even if it takes a few seconds!

ENERGY SOURCES

You are only capable of extreme physical exertion if you intake sufficient energy (sugar/starch) in the form of nourishment. If you have absorbed a sufficient amount, you achieve optimal performance capacity. Not enough causes a drop in efficiency, lack of concentration and fatigue. But with too much energy absorption there is a danger of extreme nervousness and quick exhaustion.

Available energy

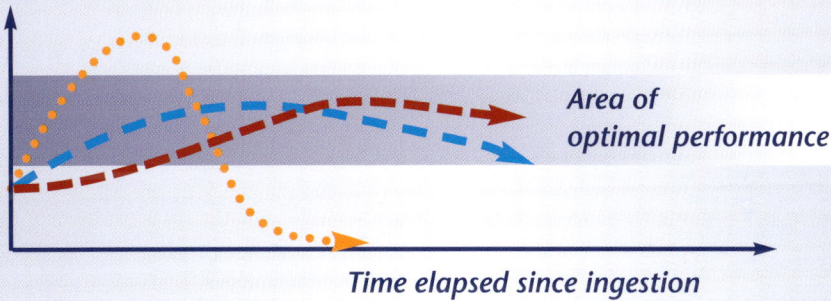

Area of optimal performance

Time elapsed since ingestion

Sweets, honey, grape sugar and sweetened beverages give you a quick burst of energy and thereby a quick performance boost. But is doesn't last long.

Milk smoothies and apples give you quick energy that is also available over a longer period of time.

Granola, whole grain products and bananas don't give you an immediate energy boost, but that energy is available over a long period of time.

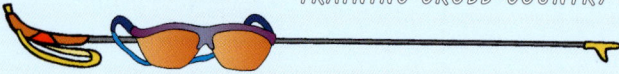

O	P	R	M	P	O	T	A	T	O	E	S	E	B
Z	U	C	C	H	I	N	I	W	L	T	M	R	I
S	V	N	M	Y	L	M	S	C	I	W	O	T	X
Q	D	M	G	Y	R	O	C	I	H	C	W	F	Z
U	M	R	E	B	M	U	C	U	C	Y	U	O	I
A	N	A	P	R	T	Y	M	O	W	O	K	T	H
S	X	N	W	S	G	V	L	R	N	M	P	A	C
H	I	A	V	K	G	I	Y	U	C	X	W	F	A
X	G	N	A	P	P	L	E	M	S	E	Z	M	N
S	N	A	R	W	H	L	E	T	T	U	C	E	I
K	Z	B	P	E	P	P	E	R	S	K	T	W	P
P	E	A	R	W	C	A	R	R	O	T	L	S	S
G	R	A	P	E	S	W	F	L	E	M	O	N	I
K	I	W	I	Y	R	R	E	B	W	A	R	T	S

Find 17 different fruits and vegetables – horizontally, vertically or diagonally, forward and backward!

Oh gee, there's always so much excitement before the start of a race!

Which is the quickest way to the restroom?

Can you trace the route?

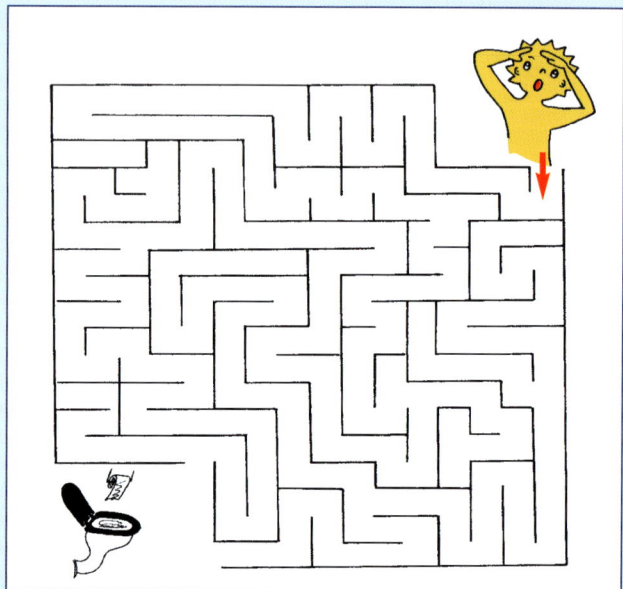

·········· 14 SOLUTIONS

Pg. 30   1. You tell the trainer that after being sick you are not yet able to do such strenuous endurance training. Surely he will start you off with some easier exercises to practice.

2. Tell him that in the last competition you did not have any trouble with the techniques for directional changes. You would rather work on your strength endurance.

Pg. 44   1.   2. Salt Lake City

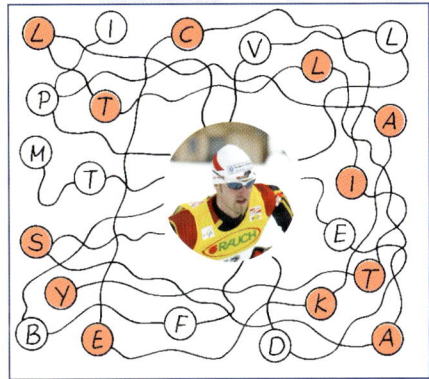

Pg. 47   **These are our suggestions:**

1. Control your speed toward the end of the downhill stretch so you don't fall in the turn.

2. The downhill stretch can be skied at full speed because the slight incline at the end will slow you down anyway, and you can use the momentum.

3. You'll stay calm and stick to your own speed strategy.

4. You try to catch up to him as quickly as possible.

5. If he catches up to you, you'll have to keep at it.

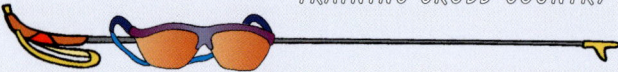

Pg. 52 1. The little bug unfortunately does not get to his sweetheart.
2. 1 – more, 2 – white, 3 – no, 4 – four

Pg. 53   **Our opinion:**

Self confidence – joy in cross-country skiing – ~~self-doubt~~ – ~~blind rage~~ – willingness to take risks – ~~impatience~~ – being laid-back – ~~fear of making mistakes~~ – ambition – desire to win – faith in one's performance – ~~pessimism~~ – ~~bad mood~~ – feeling in great form – attentiveness – concentration

Pg. 58/59

18 –15 points

You can go far with your attitude about the sport. You enjoy competing, are fair and if necessary can get over your weaker inner self. Keep it up!

14 –10 points

You have a pretty good attitude about the sport, but sometimes you are only going in first gear. With more fun and competitiveness, you could be more successful. Take the training and races seriously, be fair to the other athletes and have more fun skiing.

9 –6 points

You mostly just think about yourself! You need to work on your attitude with regard to fairness and camaraderie.

Pg. 62

S	W	I	M	M	I	N	G	T	M	O	P	L	X	H
H	F	C	R	O	S	S	C	O	U	N	T	R	Y	G
I	G	E	L	R	U	I	M	W	S	I	N	N	E	T
K	N	S	F	E	S	N	O	T	N	I	M	D	A	B
I	I	K	F	P	T	G	N	I	L	C	Y	C	I	B
N	E	A	X	E	R	E	C	C	O	S	Z	W	B	U
G	O	T	V	L	X	S	N	I	U	K	P	U	T	E
X	N	I	H	L	Z	R	Y	R	T	N	C	P	M	W
J	A	N	R	I	G	K	F	M	I	W	Z	Q	N	X
H	C	G	M	N	W	I	L	L	A	B	D	N	A	H
J	U	D	O	G	N	J	O	G	G	I	N	G	B	X
N	V	S	O	G	Y	M	N	A	S	T	I	C	S	L
T	Y	B	Y	W	L	L	A	B	Y	E	L	L	O	V
B	I	G	N	I	T	A	K	S	E	N	I	L	N	I

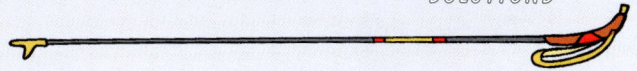

Pg. 95 **1** Arms and legs do not move diagonally here, but rather equilaterally (pace).

2 Poles are parallel as in double poling with kick.

3 The arm does not swing through, but is pulled back up much too quickly.

Pg. 99 **1** Here the poles touch down too far forward. The angle must be smaller than 90°.

2 When using the poles the skier must straighten up and feel the pressure on the ball of the foot. This skier has his upper body and knees bent.

3 The knees are bent too much and the rear is therefore much too low.

Pg. 103 **1** The poles touch down much too far forward, at an angle larger that 90°.

2 The skier stands much too erect when swinging the poles back.

3 During the kick, the poles must already be ready to push off. Here, the arms are still swinging back.

Pg. 117 **1** The movement of the poles is not parallel.

2 The skier is bent over before using the poles.

3 The position of the push-off leg is not shallow, but much too high.

Pg. 134 **1 Caution, intersection!**

Here, another run, a lift or even a road may cross the run. Sometimes there is an additional symbol or explanation with the symbol.

2 Caution, danger!

Here you must be particularly careful!

Pg. 134

Whatever you bring with you on the run you should also take back with you when you leave, or at least to the next trash receptacle! Snowman is probably not thinking about what the run will look like next summer, when there is no snow.

Pg. 142

> COME ON!
> GET A MOVE ON!

. . . . 15 LET'S TALK

DEAR CROSS-COUNTRY SKIING PARENTS

It is easy to get excited about cross-country skiing. It is a wonderful winter sport, and for many people, it is the best recreational activity in the snow. Nature and the exercise are fascinating, and together with friends it is twice as much fun.

Your child, too, has learned to ski and has fun with it. But now it is no longer satisfied with the basics and the purely recreational activity, but wants to practice cross-country skiing as a real sport. It wants to seriously train in a club and perhaps belong to a good team. Do you know why that is? Ask your child or have him show you the pages in the book that talk about motives. One thing you should understand: Someone who trains as a skier wants to be successful, start in competitions and win.

This training book focuses on young cross-country skiers in their initial years of training. It offers much information about their sport, about physical fitness and fitness training, technique, coordination and how to train right. The young people will learn to better realize their own potential and to more consciously work with their body. This does not only promote more effective training but also prevents possible under- or over-training.

The basic training and intermediate training are the same for all young skiers, regardless of whether they will later remain recreational skiers or have the goal to ski with the best in the world. For all of them, this book provides orientation and support for successful training.

All parents, siblings, grandparents and friends receive important information. In the age of television, computers and many other modern media, but many children and adolescents don't get much exposure to books, particularly specialized books. So don't expect the young athlete to immediately understand the content on his own. Use this book together with your children as a training companion, workbook and reference work.

You might occasionally be asked to help complete lists and design performance charts. Together with your young skier enjoy his progress and competitive successes.

Children and adolescents need our approval, praise and recognition. Be sympathetic on those occasions when things aren't going well. Not everyone has what it takes to be one of the best in the world.

More than anything competitive sports are fun, promote social interaction and develop ambition and perseverance. As they train together, the children and adolescents learn to overcome their weaker inner self and learn to deal with success and failure. Character traits, such as fairness, dependability, punctuality, organization, perseverance, the willingness to take risks, courage and team spirit, are cultivated and will also be useful in other areas of life.

DEAR TRAINER!

Good youth training focuses on the entire personal development of children and adolescents. It is considered a learning activity because it promotes the control and automatic control processes. It has a socializing effect because group training in particular practices social norms, rules and behavior patterns. Training for children and adolescents is stimulating and takes moods, perceptions and feelings into account.It ensures positive experiences, processes needs and wishes, and is conducted in a warm, loving and open-minded atmosphere. The young cross-country skiers are your partners in this – providing they are actively involved in the training process and have enough freedom to act. Therefore, don't view the young athletes as recipients of your orders, but as partners in the mutual training process. Tell them why which exercise is necessary when, and which workload is particularly beneficial for which training segments.

We would like to hereby hand the children a workbook that is a training companion. They can review things they have learned as well as record goals, motives and their personal performance development. Use this opportunity to read certain chapters together, assign small tasks to be done at home, fill in charts and compare results. Performance diagrams are a good way to document and follow training achievements.

Of course, no book is a substitute for the years of experience a trainer has. Also, the opinions of trainers, sports scientists and "book writers" sometimes differ. Consider this training book a training supplement and an aid in the involvement with the sport beyond the training together. A good youth trainer always thinks about how he can use ski training not only to teach about the fall line and techniques or develop physical fitness, but also how to actively involve children and adolescents in the practice and training process, so he can, aside from improving the quality of practice sessions, consciously foster the personal development of his athletes.

We wish you and your protégées continued fun and success.

. . . . PHOTO AND ILLUSTRATION CREDITS

Cover design:	Jens Vogelsang, Aachen
Illustrations:	Katrin Barth, EM. TV & Merchandising AG (Skitty)
Cover photo:	U1 – Gerhard König, Zella-Mehlis
	U4 – Hubert Brühl
Photos (inside):	E. Bechstädt, H. Dotzler, (DSV), A. Teichmann,
	R. Weitz, Regina Weitz

Page 20:   Lonocut, Hega Borisch "Staffelwechsel," Germany 1980, Sportakademie des Landessportbundes Thüringen in Bad Blankenburg (Germany).

Tempora on paper, Hans Erni "Cross-country Skiing," Switzerland 1983, IOC Chateau de Vidy Lausanne.

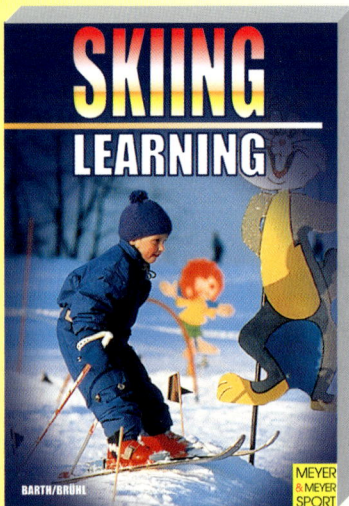

Barth/Brühl

Learning ... Skiing

This book is written for children just beginning to ski. The little snowman and his friend, the tiger Skitty, offer comprehensible and humorous guidance for children's first attempts on skis, to successfully skiing downhill. In addition, the children learn interesting facts about winter sports, snow, equipment, a healthy lifestyle, and safety precautions.

136 pages, full-color print
37 photos, 240 illustrations
Paperback, 5 3/4" x 8 1/4"
ISBN 1-84126-154-8
£ 9.95 UK/$ 14.95 US
$ 20.95 CDN/€ 14.95

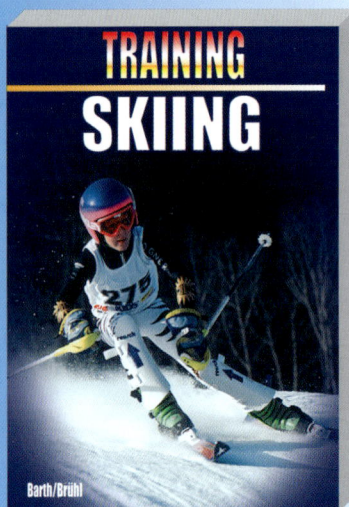

Barth/Brühl

Training ... Skiing

"Training Skiing" focuses on children and adolescents who want to train for alpine skiing. The question "Training correctly – but how?" is answered in an age-appropriate manner. The young athletes find out how to learn the right techniques step by step, how to recognize mistakes and how to correct them. The "little Snowman" and his friend, the tiger "Skitty", are amusing companions throughout the book; they offer numerous tips on training and competing, as well as exercises to do at home.

136 pages, full-color print
30 photos and 150 illustrations
Paperback, 5 3/4" x 8 1/4"
ISBN 1-84126-174-2
c. £ 9.95 UK/$ 14.95 US
$ 20.95 CDN/€ 14.90

MEYER & MEYER SPORT

MEYER & MEYER distribution@m-m-sports.com • www.m-m-sports.com

An/CrossCountrySkiing 6/06